No Life

for a

Lady

No Life
for a
Lady

by

Lotta Dempsey

Musson Book Company
Don Mills, Ontario

First published 1976 by
Musson Book Company

Canadian Cataloguing in Publication Data

Dempsey, Lotta
  No life for a lady

ISBN 0-7737-0029-3

1. Dempsey, Lotta. I. Title.

PN4913.D38A3   070.9'2'4   C76-017011-8

ISBN 0-7737-0029-3

Printed and bound in Canada
1 2 3 4 5 THB 80 79 78 77 76

To Martin Goodman, Editor-in-Chief of *The Toronto Star*, whose gift of time, without strings, made this venture possible.

And to Borden Spears, my top-of-class managing editor, whose gift of listening brought it to conclusion.

Then to D., without whom none of it would have mattered.

Preface

One of the stories Lotta Dempsey tells about herself concerns the time when her husband and one of their sons were listening, in their Toronto home, to the radio description of a Royal visit to Ottawa. The announcer said that a woman reporter, following the Queen in a press launch, had just fallen into the Ottawa river. "That," said her husband with resignation, "will be your mother."

Readers of this book will quickly become aware that the anecdote rings false on two counts, for both of which Lotta herself is responsible. First, she did *not* fall into the river; she walked in, albeit imprudently, as the fastest method of getting ashore with her story. Second, in every story about herself, Lotta is the victim, the fall guy, the hapless innocent confounded. As all who know her will testify, it is a characterization far short of the truth about a totally professional journalist whom her peers place in the front rank of her craft.

You will not get the other kind of story from her. To get it, you would have to interview the great and near-great, the presidents and personages, and the host of more obscure people, no less interesting and important to her, who have opened their hearts to this extraordinary newspaperwoman in the confidence that she would not let them down.

She never has let them down. Nor — and this is the mark of a journalist's integrity — has she let her newspaper and its readers down. Despite occasional forays into radio, television, and magazine work, Lotta is first, last, and always a newspaperwoman. She is among the great ones because she is inspired by an insatiable curiosity, a concern for people before abstract issues, and a passionate devotion to truth and justice.

Though publishers have pursued her for years, this is her first book. She has been too busy writing in the newspapers about others and too diffident to claim the stage for herself.

No Life for a Lady is only incidentally the story of Lotta Dempsey. It has a wider compass — it is the record of an era as seen through the eyes of a reporter who was privileged to be where great events were happening, to explore the minds of those who made them happen, and to interpret them for the rest of us.

But turn the page, and let her tell it. No one can do it better.

Borden Spears
Senior Editor
The Toronto Star

No Life

for a

Lady

Foreword

My father was a man of fixed ideas.

One was that young women out walking miniature poodles tended to be fancy fillies up to no good.

Another concerned the dangers of teaching boys to play piano. "They end in houses of ill repute or as sissies," was his considered contention. "Sissies" covered a variety of imbalances and frailties in males.

Perhaps his greatest *idée fixe* involved his only child. No daughter of Alex Dempsey, ramrod-straight, white-aproned proprietor of the little Bon Ton Fruit Store on Edmonton's Jasper Avenue near First Street, was going to be a newspaper reporter if he could help it.

"It's no life for a lady," he echoed our long-time weekly char Annie, when I pleaded my cause. My mother, being younger than springtime (it was a Trudeau-Margaret romance), kept silent.

I think she secretly yearned for the excitement and upheaval, even by proxy, of the adventures of those looseliving, roistering loungers and loafers my father considered journalists to be. ("A grown man going around with a pencil and paper sticking his nose into other people's business and piddling with a typewriter," scorned this hardy son of toil.)

Admittedly, in his small emporium halfway between the two daily newspapers, the *Edmonton Journal* and the *Edmonton Bulletin*, he had a fair vantage point. Of course, the ones he didn't see at his closing time around midnight were the majority, such as accountants and shoe salesmen, who went straight home to wives and kids. Or some accountants and shoe salesmen.

He did not know, either, that I had been subverted early by one of his most respected friends, a school principal. This gentleman, offering help with some balky high school algebra, would receive me and my math books in the sanctuary of his small study, his wife and my mother innocently chatting outside. In his feckless secret past, Dr. William Todd had been a newspaperman.

So no sooner were we settled than I coaxed him into reminiscences . . . lurid court trials, murders, morgues, disasters, jails, scalawaggery of the high and mighty, cupidity of the debased, in the gutsy, go-after-'em days of the Barbary Coast.

It was from Bill I learned the who-what-when-where-why rudiments of reporting for the press; "journalese" that lost me marks on essays but won newspaper contests; the high-voltage charge of watching the world go 'round in all its vagaries . . . and seeing people read *your* version in the streets.

Bill was to be followed by a long line of enchanters and enchantresses with whom I worked or tilted in the business, vying for the tip-toe excitement of a good assignment or lead.

I was to find for myself the mounting pitch of every day, as one after another edition came wet-inked off the press; the unmatchable satisfaction of a by-line; the warts of biggies concealed by their public images; the simplicity of the rare and truly great.

I was to learn the deceptive joy of an expense account, when scrutinized in the after-glow of business office judgement. And of an airline ticket to romantic places with notice too short for so much as a toothbrush.

Ah, the magic of a press card, which delivers closed-circuit contact with kings, queens, and princes; thieves and robber barons; politicians, prostitutes, scientists, labour bosses, poets, promoters, actors, musicians, dancers; Hollywood and Broadway stars; Ottawa, Washington, and London government mandarins. Ringside seats at combustible events from Victoria to Newfoundland; Tuktoyaktuk to Caracas; the whole galaxy and gambit of the life situation.

I satisfied my father by taking my first-class teaching certificate ("so you'll have a respectable trade to fall back on") and taught eight weeks in a little country school house at Four Corners, Alberta. Then, on a glorious September day at the age of 18, eager to climb Parnassus or explore caverns of the farthest seas, I went to work in the editorial department of the *Edmonton Journal*. The managing editor had simply wearied of me lurking in the wings. My first assignment was a meeting of the local Children's Aid Society, my weekly salary, $17.50.

Looking back from my present post as columnist and feature writer for *The Toronto Star*, Canada's largest daily and fourth on the continent, I also realize somewhat to my surprise that I was, as a woman, something of a pioneer. I was too involved, too happy, too busy falling in and out of adventure, chasing down celebrities, covering disasters and other sadder segments of existence to notice. I recall Sinclair Lewis remarking once, when his wife Dorothy Thompson went to work for the National Broadcasting Company, that she simply disappeared into the network and never was seen or heard of after. I disappeared into the press. There was time out for an architect husband, children, the good family things, and the tumultuous life that two peripatetic professionals can sometimes impose on their toddling innocents.

I defected for a considerable spell to a magazine, becoming for a stranger-than-fiction period editor-in-chief of *Chatelaine*; went to the Wartime Prices and Trade Board in Ottawa to do public relations when my husband was in the army in World War II; dabbled in radio (a news editor and commentator for the Canadian Broadcasting Corporation; master of ceremonies for one of the first quiz shows in Canada) and television.

But I came back to my first love, the world of giant rolling presses, make-up men and compositors, unflappable press photographers, irascible city editors. The thrill of the kill with a scoop over rivals; suicidal despair at a lost story or betrayal; the triumph of breaking a big story first. The corny thing called printer's ink.

My confrères long have been the best company I know in a world that is frenetic, disastrous, divine . . . but never dull or lacklustre. I wouldn't trade my experiences and expectations for all the oil in Saudi Arabia, the acupuncture needles of China, or the Rockefeller zillions.

I hope you enjoy reading *No Life for a Lady* as much as I enjoy living it.

P.S. I failed the algebra exam.

One

.

It would have been difficult to explain to the Duke of Windsor or Mike Pearson, Eleanor Roosevelt, or, say, Noel Coward. Here was a reporter talking to them, getting to know them, because a crazy kid sent her. And how could I point out to the little French prostitute, when I walked the streets beside her at two o'clock of a drizzly morning in Paris's notorious Place Pigalle, that it was the kid's idea.

All of us have crazy kids tucked away under our adult skins — the children we once were, dreaming into the future and pushing us to act out their fantasies. Very early on I knew I wanted to pack every waking minute of what I sensed to be a short life with excitement and adventure, to reach beyond my small city, where you always found somebody's aunt or cousin beckoning to a seat on the streetcar and where there were rarely new shops or showplaces to explore. I wanted to live in a world of strangers and change, to find out as much about everything and everybody as I could, and to put it all down. To be a newspaper reporter.

When I made that decision I was still an eager, rangy towhead with a grin, bangs, and braids looped at the back and tied with big hair ribbons. As an only child (a baby brother died when I was five), I was encouraged so shamelessly by my parents to recite, play pieces on the piano, and read my verses to suffering friends and relatives, I had few social inhibitions until my teens.

Everybody's adolescence is terrible, I know, but the peculiar cross I bore in my teens seemed to me more terrible than most. I've never quite forgiven my parents for calling me Lotta. It was for my mother's only sister, Charlotte, who had been named for her aunt, Carlotta. I was simply, as legally registered, Lotta. It must have been quite evident from my size at birth that I was going to be big, like my father, rather than small-boned and dainty, like my mother. The name Lotta Dempsey was a whip scourge in high school because I was a long-legger and pretty good at basketball (jumping centre, naturally). Jack Dempsey was then a world-famous prize fighter. I leave to your imagination the shouts of "Here comes a lotta Dempsey!" and "Shoot, Jack!" from the male gym gallery, especially when my fellow players were being hailed by such endearing terms as Skinny Kinney and Freckles Fuller. Ah, the tear-stained pillows on the evenings of triumphant games. At Victoria High we could beat every girls' team, including the University of Alberta squad, except the Edmonton Grads. (We were their favourite practice adversaries as they went off to world championships.) And you know who the boys like Clarence Campbell and Wacky Bennett and Ronnie Martland (now Chief Justice Ronald Martland) took out? Bitsy curly heads such as Millie B. (I met Millie years later in a Toronto Eaton's washroom, and she had turned into a satisfactorily dumpy frump. But how was I to know, at 16?)

Through public and high school, I worked after four (not very hard) in my father's little fruit store, the Bon Ton. I had to start at the bottom and earn my way up to behind-the-counter service, where I learned early from my father an important tenet of my later journalistic years. "Giving the customer what he came in for isn't salesmanship," he used to say. "It's talking him into something he didn't know he had in mind." Often in a routine interview or story, it's the unpremeditated something you coax from your subject that makes the headline.

I also learned at a somewhat tender age, when occasionally tending store alone at nights, how to handle drunks and smart alecks. A useful skill ever since.

The Bon Ton set the pattern of my future in many ways. Starting at the bottom meant working in the back room, where the crates of fruit and vegetables were delivered. Mr. Morrison, the only clerk, pried the slats off the wooden boxes while I washed slimy grubs and gritty sand out of lettuce and spinach and searched stalks of bananas for errant tarantulas. I shined apples and sorted berries and other perishables for mouldies. My father was meticulous about the quality of his merchandise.

The back room was a window to a world known to few of the other kids at McKay Avenue Public School, kids I sometimes envied a little because their fathers were doctors or accountants or civil servants. (One of my father's most persistent drives was to live in the "right" part of town, and so he built our little bungalow cheek by jowl with residences of more formally educated people. He could have had a bigger, cheaper place among many of his friends, mostly fine tradespeople, in the "east" end.) While female classmates went home to their mothers and learned to cook, sew, and clean house, I was with my father, and *we* went home to mother — a rare privilege, I now realize, although I never was properly housebroken. Mother carried the distaff department solo.

Because holiday periods were those of our biggest business, I never even selected a Christmas present for anyone but my mother until after the Bon Ton had gone awash with

3

the deluge of the Depression, like so many small businesses. Christmas Eve we worked until well after midnight. That was when late shoppers came in for the big boxes of candy and baskets of fruit for their girls and families, price no object. I was probably the only child in my neighbourhood who had to be shaken awake, really shaken, on Christmas morning.

So I learned to break string without hurting my finger, make change like lightning, figure from our secret wholesale price code how much I could mark down an item. I knew about keeping plug chewing tobacco and pouches of the pipe stuff moist with cut-up apples and could make expert judgement on a variety of melons, potatoes, cabbages, and squash. I have frequently since astounded grocers by predicting almost to an ounce the weight of produce I have bought before it touches the scales. But what one did with all these foodstuffs once they were in the kitchen I only learned, with great difficulty and many mishaps, much later in life.

In the office, just off the back room, my father used to sit late at nights on his high stool under a goose-neck desk lamp, wearing his green eyeshade and sleeve-holders, working over bills and charge accounts. Here I learned, every Saturday morning, to talk to a list of preferred customers on the telephone, taking orders, promoting merchandise that had just arrived, and helping Mr. Morrison fill the cartons for Bert, the delivery boy. It was good training for a reporter, for accuracy was important. God help the young Dempsey, with the big white butcher's apron tied around her still unbudded chest, if Judge Scott's or Senator Griesbach's wife got McIntosh Reds instead of Baldwins or brussels sprouts when asparagus was indicated. (As a cub reporter on the *Edmonton Journal*, I still worked in the store Saturdays. Not infrequently I was horribly embarrassed by some such estimable lady shouting over to the press table at a convention or parliamentary reception that I had forgotten the radishes or sent navel oranges instead of "Japs".)

Lotta at kindergarten age with her pet dog Peaches.

Lotta's mother, then in her mid-twenties.

In early years I rode the delivery wagon beside Bert while Ginger, the roan, stopped almost automatically at the well-known homes of Edmonton swells. As I helped carry in bundles, I got my first look at small-city grandeur through the kitchen . . . and sometimes sneaked through to see what a drawing room or a conservatoire was like. There were times later, as a front-door-welcomed journalist, I could have given interesting insight into below-stairs conditions and maid's quarters.

But the back room itself held great charm. By cocking a sharp little ear under the hair ribbons, I listened to Big Tom and Tiny, Scotty or Irish, all hefty six-footers and more in their blue police uniforms, swapping crime gossip and news. I was careful never to reveal to my gentle mother details of these conversations, but they were probably the basis for much of my later interest in courtrooms and bordellos, jails and morgues, rescue homes and flophouses. I also acquired considerable awareness of the perfidies and peccadillos of some of our leading churchgoers, politicians, and community leaders. It engendered a healthy scepticism and a background in human behaviour that was to be useful when later I delved into some of the big scandals of our time.

Knowing the police, of course, had its hazards. In an early teen-age flush of love, one evening a boy friend had borrowed his father's flivver. After seeing a movie we parked with another couple in a local lovers' lane and engaged in a little innocuous (in the light of current practice) petting. Suddenly a flashlight blinded me. It was Tiny of the morality squad.

"Lotta Dempsey!" he bellowed. "What would your father say? Young man, get that engine cranked and deliver this girl home, and you'd better be there in fifteen minutes!"

The other great bonanza of the back room, which accounted in no small measure for my diligence as daddy's little helper, was that it was just across the lane from the stage-door entrance to one of the two local vaudeville houses, the Pantages Theatre. (The other was the

Orpheum.) Here actors and clowns, dancers, singers, acrobats, aspiring chorines and fading mezzo sopranos, and trainers with animal acts (including elephants) would stroll and smoke and exercise between turns and performances. Harry Crossley, treasurer of the theatre, and his wife Ted, who sold tickets, were friends of my parents, and so I had carte blanche out front and used it often.

What none of them knew was how much time I spent backstage in dressing-rooms, watching grease paint applied, questioning prop men and musicians, and sitting in (as observer) on dice and poker games. Here I saw my first woman smoking a cigarette and my first baby nested in a trunk. I also sensed the warmth of many of the family and buddy relationships and learned about the hard work, constant practice, and the sweat behind the sweet smell of success in the making of a pro.

Many of the famed comedians of a later day played the Pantages — Jack Benny, Red Skelton, Al Jolson, Georgie Jessel, Milton Berle, George Burns and Gracie Allen, Eddie Cantor, Fred Allen and Portland Hoffa. And the crazy kid who loved them then has sent me out hunting them down, in Hollywood and London and New York and Las Vegas, ever since.

I learned other things in the Bon Ton and from my father. When the lieutenant-governor was brought ceremoniously to the back room, as he frequently was, to inspect some fresh arrival of fitting quality, he called my father Mr. Dempsey and my father called him Your Honour. Other favoured clients were given this special treatment — judges, medicos, legislators — and they and my father carried through this ritual with the grace of a French minuet. My father also called by their surnames the wonderful Chinese vegetable growers, who brought a rich treasure of good produce to our store — Mr. Chan, Mr. Chung, and Mr. Lee. Until the chef at the Prince Edward Hotel became his friend and with his wife often visited our home, my father called him Mr.

Montrose. Then it was Monty, but not for me. I never was told that Mr. Montrose was black, any more than it would be pointed out each of our friends was different from the others in some ways, until a classmate noted it. I never heard my father call any grown man "boy" or "you" or "son". As time passed and I grew older, I found that the standards of the Bon Ton and my home were not always those of the world at large. I learned something of the snobbery of even a small city, when the grocer's daughter and the lawyer's daughter and the doctor's daughter grow older and lose their childhood innocence of status.

This, too, may have had something to do with my finding so comfortable and fulfilling my present trade which, for some reason, breaks through all the pecking orders. To be in the fourth estate is, by and large, to enjoy a state of grace among the righteous . . . unless, or until, they fall by the wayside. And who cares what the baddies think about you?

My father never singled out people of our town as worthy of emulation because they were wealthy. He admired achievement and brains and quality. "Look at so-and-so," he would say of some such worthy. "He's smart, and he's got class."

So it isn't really surprising that my first and long-time idol, of whom my father had never heard, should be someone who was very smart and who certainly had class. It was a long way from the Bon Ton to getting to know Noel Coward. But I made it.

Two

"Are you still here?" Noel Coward said softly, touching my shoulder. "It's frightfully late."

He had come up quietly from the back of the darkened theatre and paused where I was sitting alone, my gaze riveted on the brightly lighted scene on stage. I was so involved I simply nodded and answered with what seemed an obvious point.

"Of course, Mr. Coward. We haven't got the coronation number right yet."

He smiled, the kindest smile I had ever seen, eyes tired behind horn-rimmed glasses. Then, soberly, in those clipped British tones, "Of course. So you wait and we'll see what we can do. Be sure not to try to get back to the hotel alone. Someone will fetch you up there."

It was well after three in the morning and late for a dress rehearsal, even at Boston's midtown Colonial Playhouse, setting for so may pre-Broadway tryouts. They *were* having trouble with the coronation scene, as well as other aspects of the mixed English and American cast for *The Girl Who Came to Supper*. It was Coward's and Harry Kurnitz's musical adaptation of the Terence Rattigan play, *The Sleeping Prince*, which had fared well when filmed with Marilyn Monroe and Laurence Olivier.

Somehow it just wasn't welding, despite the crisp Coward flavour and good music. José Ferrer and Florence Henderson seemed very American in the leads (Florence Henderson apple-pie, doughnut-dunking American, to me) and hard put to catch the fragile, knife-edge timing and inflections so essential in a Coward-stamped work.

On the other hand, the two featured players Coward had brought from London were unmistakably British. One was the ebullient Tessie O'Shea, toast of the music halls and supper clubs of the British Isles; the other, seasoned Irene Browne, to play a very regal Queen Mother. The division was so sharp that each pair might have wandered from the stage doors of other productions into this setting in error.

And what was I doing so involved out front, day after day, night after night, from bare rehearsal hall to opening performance? Fulfilling the dream of a teen-ager in Edmonton, when I discovered Noel Coward and friends in a magazine (Frank Crowninshield's glossy, literate *Vanity Fair*). I determined I would one day come to know this witty darling of the roaring 'twenties, this effervescent sparkler in the bleak and dirty 'thirties. Somewhere out there was a fabulous world of beautiful people in glamorous clothes doing lovely things so different from my little prairie city. Those people didn't wear long underwear, moccasins, toques, and Hudson's Bay blanket coats from November until March.

After I came East, the dream seemed closer, for people in Toronto were theatre-conscious and in touch with London and New York, Broadway and the West End, where stars like Coward played. But it wasn't until my honeymoon in New York in 1936 (I was too busy making ends meet in Toronto to get there the year I spent in the city before marrying) that I had my first audience encounter with the Coward magic. Noel Coward and Gertrude Lawrence were playing in *Tonight at 8.30*. From the second balcony (young architects like my husband were as poverty-stricken as everyone else in those still Depression days) I watched, entranced.

"Will you please see if you can get backstage and ask Mr. Coward for an autographed photograph?" I asked my bridegroom. After murmuring that he must have married some kind of nut and was this the beginning of . . . he set forth at intermission. Somehow he managed to get the autograph. What did I want it for? To keep to show Mr. C. some day when I finally got to know him.

Some day had to wait until 1963. By then I was a feature writer and columnist for *The Toronto Star*, Canada's largest daily, and had done a number of assignments for the entertainment editor, a remarkable intellectual and critic, Nathan Cohen. Cohen had sent me to Montreal, Ottawa, New York, Hollywood, and Las Vegas. A warm perceptive human being, he was aware of my adulation of Coward, often teasing me about such devotion to someone he considered a mini-great at best. But he also knew I was a professional and could be trusted not to sound (as I do now) like a star-struck schoolgirl when I wrote about him. Besides, Coward was my one Achilles heel in an otherwise fairly sound assessment of the people, places, and things I reported.

Thus one day Nate mooched over to my corner of the city room, sat down and, characteristically, put his feet on my desk. "There's a play going into rehearsal in Boston and coming on to Toronto for a pre-Broadway opening," he said innocently. "Would you like to spend a couple of weeks there and see it through the whole routine? You've never done that."

Always eager to be off on any adventure, I nodded quickly. (I've had editors complain that one of their problems was to keep my seat in contact with my desk for any recordable length of time.) What was the play? Who was in it? Why was the *Star* so . . . ?

Cohen lifted an authoritative hand and waited a moment. "An English minor leaguer, Noel Coward, is involved, and he's coming over to help put on the production. Now, I'll want you to file . . . ."

So here I was in Boston, just a few hours from the opening, after practically living in the theatre from that first day of rehearsal. I wasn't going to desert the Master (as everyone called Coward affectionately) in these early morning hours, fighting through problems. I had become, in my own mind, part and parcel of the whole operation.

This is something of what I wrote about those days in the *Star*:

> However early I arrived at the theatre each day, the quiet man with the slightly hunched shoulders was in his seat on the aisle, seventh row centre; tweed jacket and ascot meticulously in character, crinkled face all but enveloped in large horn-rims.
>
> Coward would sit hour after hour at rehearsal, bent forward with just a perceptible tap of the finger, or making notes on a pad. He always waited for breaks before offering suggestions, and never did so directly, but always through the young American director, Joe Layton.
>
> On occasion, Coward would disappear into the orchestra pit, head bent over sheets of music with one musician or another. His approach to all those except close friends was what might be described as charmingly affable but remote. Mr. Coward does not, one feels, make friends on impulse, any more than in his enormously well-disciplined and organized life he does other things without careful thought and planning.

His voice never rose, his gestures always were controlled, and, in a catch-as-catch-can clad group, many in jeans and sweaters, he was every inch the properly-turned-out English gentleman. I couldn't imagine him creased, mussed or unpressed.

I had achieved considerable rapport with most of the cast, except Florence Henderson, later a highly successful television performer. I found her dull as an interviewee and seemingly lacking in warmth as a person, an opinion not unshared in this company. She talked interminably about husband, children, and her religious beliefs. In her role in the play, she seemed to me to lack that strange combination of sexual magnetism and innocence that characterized Marilyn Monroe, which had made her so right for the role of the little chorus girl who comes to supper with the prince and, expecting to spend a night of dalliance, wins his love.

José Ferrer was pleasant when I could pry away the young admirers long enough to talk with him. I think he felt a little uncomfortable in the role, possibly because he couldn't achieve the right communication with Henderson and had one of his best and most sympathetic numbers, "Middle Age", chopped early on.

Tessie O'Shea, later to become well known in America on television, stage, and screen (*The Russians Are Coming*, etc.) was in this country for the first time, although she was by then a household name in Britain, much of Africa, and Australia. That beginning rehearsal day she burst in on a largely unprepared cast with all her full-blown warmth, wearing the dilapidated rose-trimmed straw hat she would use in the musical (for good luck — no one else had a smidge of stage costume). She tore into a rather stodgy scene like the merry burst of a calliope. Admittedly, her whole part was a little out of key with the rest of the play (it was an impromptu street concert, with chorus and dancers, outside the palace), but suddenly everything came alive.

After the opening that night in Boston, no one knew whether I should be invited to join the party. The Master decided these things, and he was known not to look too kindly on reporters being present at such times. There *is* something sort of vulture-like about a reporter watching performers endure the waiting while triumph or disaster is being spelled out on critical typewriters, and so I respected his feelings. I had no intention of intruding. But as we passed in the lobby, Mr. Coward came over. "Ah, our friend from Canada. We'll want you with us."

What we said or did I can't recall. It was all nervously inconsequential. But the reviews were wonderful. Coward moved from player to player with words of congratulation, and we went wearily to bed in the early dawn.

The axe fell in Toronto, where Nathan Cohen was, as so often, more keyed to casting errors, audience climate, and odds on durability. *The Girl Who Came to Supper* faltered on to New York and died a consumptive death.

Yet it was in Toronto that I came to know Coward in a deeper sense. I could tell him now about the crazy kid in the Bon Ton Fruit Store. He had come from very simple beginnings himself and was a good listener. He never put down the vulnerable. He couldn't believe I had even seen him in a perfectly ghastly film, where he played a cadaver, walking out of the sea covered in long strands of seaweed. The movie was called *The Scoundrel,* and he had been very young. It wasn't until I was invited alone to his suite in the King Edward Hotel, a place scattered with books from the suitcase of all sorts of reading matter he always carried, that I brought out the autographed picture from 1936.

"Yes, you must have the matching one now, Lotta," he said. This time it was more personally inscribed.

"You know, Mr. Coward," I ventured, *"The Girl Who Came to Supper* would have been a marvellous party with you and Gertrude Lawrence." The luminous Lawrence was long since dead.

Coward nodded. "Yes, Gertie. And I imagine I wrote myself into the prince part. One does that you know. It would have been fine for me, younger."

He went on to say that when he had gone to Buckingham Palace with the songs he had written for this play, the royal family loved them. I knew he was a favourite, especially with the Queen Mother and Princess Margaret.

"You mustn't write this now," he said, "but the Queen Mum sat on a cushion on the floor and hummed and clapped. Princess Margaret chorded with me at the piano. She's good."

We talked of his plays, and he mentioned *The Vortex* as his strongest, most serious achievement. "But they wanted lighter things from me."

I dared to chide him for having created so much of his own image. He was tagged with his lyric from "Credo", a mocking but sadly beautiful song that was Judy Garland's favourite — "All I ever had was a talent to amuse." "And why," I asked, "would you let Elyot, in *Private Lives,* say of that haunting number, 'Some Day I'll Find You', how potent cheap music can be?"

Through a long and varied career in the press, my sights have been trained on real-life drama, tragedy and comedy, oftener than on make-believe. I know the difference. Those days with Noel Coward had elements of both. For some reason, they were among the tenderest of my experience. A youthful ambition fulfilled? Realization of the vista of a brave new world? Sharing a period of which the playwright would himself have said, life could indeed be bittersweet? Perhaps.

Yet in retrospect, I see Noel Coward would have fitted into the back room of the Bon Ton, among the special company my father received there, as gracefully as he did in Buckingham Palace, being knighted by his queen . . . .

He was a very civilized human being. And such a bloody gentleman.

Three

The first four newspaper offices I worked in had no women's washrooms on the editorial floor.

Who needed them? When the *Edmonton Journal*, the *Edmonton Bulletin,* and Toronto's *Globe and Mail* and *Star* buildings were designed, the social editor and the managing editor's secretary tended to be the sole skirted inhabitants of otherwise all-male bastions. The social editor was out a lot, attending such affairs as pink teas. So, when not at her typewriter, the social editor could use facilities in some of the town's most prestigious bathrooms. At the office, with the managing editor's secretary, she would make the up- or downstairs' trip to the advertising, want ad, circulation, or business offices. That's where the women were, in low-pay service jobs. And that, naturally, was where the women's washrooms were. Who was going to install a john in the reporters' haven for two mere jills?

I subject you to this somewhat scatological aspect of pioneering for women in journalism because it is a telling indication of the prevalent attitude towards woman staffers. When I first came to *The Toronto Star* as a columnist and feature writer, we females, although beginning to form a visible minority, had to make a very long journey, even after descending a flight of back stairs, to the business office. I think I helped the paths of progress a little there on a Sunday when I was working. The then managing editor Charles Templeton brought in his two small children.

"Lotta, take my daughter to the washroom, will you?" he said, and went off a few steps to the men's with the boy. I did, indeed. And I went a very, very long route around, moving at a pace quite brisk for small legs. I'm ordinarily kindly disposed to children and rarely treat them roughly, but I had a message to convey through this one.

"Tell daddy," I said when we had made the wearying journey back, "what a distance girls have to go to wee wee in these nice, big, shiny offices."

Facilities were later installed and, of course, the beautiful new *Star* building at the foot of Toronto's Yonge Street has admirable women's restrooms, including carpeted lounges with easy chairs and settees.

When, at 18, I got my first reporting job on the *Edmonton Journal*, I wouldn't have cared if I'd had to use an outdoor privy off the truck-loading lot. I'd just come from one, anyway, in my brief spasm of teaching at the Four Corners rural school near Ferintosh, Alberta. From there I'd brought pupils home occasionally to my parents' place. They were sturdy, skilled young farm children who could plough, milk, and help with haying and calving, but who had to be taught about the wonders and the intricacies of indoor plumbing. One later advantage of my own early disciplining was that on many male-oriented assignments, as in military manoeuvres, army camps, aboard mine sweepers, and at internment camps, I wasn't given to whining about a place to sit if there was only a place to stand. Not being a bother to the male world often gets you farther than, say, making out with a superior. This latter technique can get you only so far, I have observed over the years; then you may find that, having come in the front door, you've worked right through to an exit at the back.

The Toronto Star did at least hire woman reporters earlier than most papers. On one visit from Edmonton, when I made a job-hunting call on Mr. J. Harry Smith, city editor of *The Mail and Empire* (later to merge with the *Globe* and become *The Globe and Mail*), he foreshortened my eager recital of experience and competence with a curt, "I haven't any women reporters here and I don't want any."

I got my job on the *Journal*, I think, because I had been bombarding the paper with offerings from public school on through high and normal (teacher training). These included my poems. Often I brought carefully pencilled if not over-whelmingly newsworthy items in personally, because I loved the newspaper office.

Nowadays there are excellent training schemes for young reporters — schools of journalism, summer job programs in big dailies like the *Star*, where those suspected of ability and rapport are brought in with salaries while they learn during summer holidays and given special on-the-job tuition and guidance. Many staffers now come from university and college graduation classes when they have put in their time. But mine was the rough-and-tumble, learn-by-doing school where discipline sometimes took the form of a thrown ink-well or a knuckle-rap with a ruler. I was under the anything but tender care of a Simon Legree (as he seemed then) city editor. My first confrontation with such a one, by name MacPherson, was an early and memorable happening.

I had been taken into the Women's Department under the direction of an able but stern maiden newswoman named Edna Kells, who was developing something more than a catalogue of social doings, recipes, and fashions. But the social column was still a must.

Mr. MacPherson was barely aware, if at all, of the new girl in the sheltered little office corner where Miss Kells and I laboured, boxed off from the rest of the city room. But when she took ill, I decided our social column could do with a little upgrading. I just happened to have written a poem the night before, on a day when I found myself short of time to telephone for any lengthy chronicle of the comings, goings, and social soirées of the upper crust. So I sent the poem out to the composing room, marked "lead-all, social".

The paper appeared, and I was sitting back basking in the beauty of my handiwork when I became aware of a dark, foreboding figure (he seemed eight feet tall and very wide) filling the doorway of my little cubicle.

"Who, may I be so bold as to ask, is L.C.D.?" Mac-Pherson queried in a tone so gentle it was far more disturbing than any of the bellows I had frequently heard across the city room.

"I am," I said. "Those are my initials. Lotta Caldwell Dempsey . . . sir."

"Oh."

His large, hairy hand reached over and lifted the page from my desk. There proceeded then one of the most crescendos readings of any of my works, or anyone else's, I have ever heard.

He started in almost a whisper, dwelling on each word:

> So many little things each day
> I have to do along the way
> That I must go.
> My life work means such little deeds
> One flower, perchance, plucked from the weeds
> And made to grow.

Reporters began to gather. He cleared his throat and went on in louder tones:

I never had a chance to make
A name of honour, or to take
The victor's wreath.
Unornamented is my brow.
Before my fame no masses bow
Or call me chief.

By now members of the newsroom were standing several
male rows deep, including copy boys and printers' devils. A
proofreader and a grimy-aproned make-up man from the
back shop had joined the throng. Word was spreading that
MacPherson was about to blow, and that, in full eruption,
was a terrible and thunderous sight to witness.

The editor looked around, turned back to watch me begin
my downwards slide in my chair, and went on, his voice
rising in a truly climactic basso:

And yet, when as the days pass by
My labours with the trifles lie
And little deeds,
May I remember, Father mine,
The mighty oak, the fruitful vine
Were tiny seeds.

By now he had caught the attention of the managing
editor, who moved out of his office towards the fringe.

"Gentlemen," boomed MacPherson, his voice a mixture
of agony and anger, "this is an offering ladled out to the
readers of this great family journal today. Small, helpless
children are innocently tracing and lisping these words.
Women, worn with child-bearing, cooking, and cleaning,
find *this* as they search for some window to the march of
events in the great world outside. Men, home weary from the
field and the factory (there were very few factories in Edmonton at that time), seeking knowledge and information,
eager to broaden their horizons, paid hard-earned money to
read *this*!"

He waved the page about. "Any comment?"

"Yes," said Mr. Morrison, the managing editor, trying to keep the laughter out of his voice. "It's easier to read than some of the tripe coming out of those typewriters under the pretence of being news. And there are no typos. Leave the kid alone, Mac. I'll handle it."

We came to a kindly but firm understanding. I would save my verses for a later time and place and a more receptive audience. Meanwhile, we would be simple and ordinary and down-to-earth.

"Perhaps," said this remarkable human being, "you need to get out and into something more challenging."

And I did — the hotel beat, the rubber-chicken and green-pea luncheon circuit, and interviews. Interviewing was, immediately, what I loved most, because it meant satisfying an insatiable curiosity, asking people all sorts of things and writing stories about them.

This practice has become so all-pervasive that over the years I have frequently been ticked off by members of my family when, say, on a holiday or at a social gathering, I pinion someone and start questioning. It can be baffling, I admit, if the pinionee isn't aware of your calling. It happened not long ago at a party, when I was so fascinated by the island lore I was drawing out of the acting Governor of St. Lucia in the West Indies, I was not conscious that the hostess was growing uneasy. Time was passing, and my daughter-in-law overheard someone mention that no one could take his leave until His Excellency did. Food and drink could well have been running short. So my worthy acquired relative came firmly over, led me away, and released the victim — *and* the hosts and guests. "How often must I tell you?" she said, with an affectionate sigh.

By and large, I've found few individuals on the right side of the law who didn't enjoy being drawn out by an eager listener. And everyone in my experience has at least one good story in a lifetime.

One of my earliest teachers in the art of interviewing was a young woman, crisp in tailored suit and white shirtwaist with neatly drawn-back dark hair, who came to Edmonton on a national tour. She was newly appointed director of the Dominion Council of Child and Family Welfare, a precedent-shattering operation she had been instrumental in setting up. Her name was Charlotte Whitton, and she was later to become one of Canada's best-known women and long-time fiery little mayor of Ottawa.

I was not yet being entrusted with official visitors on important national business, but a sudden shortage of staff the day of her arrival caused Mr. MacPherson to look in my direction. He sighed resignedly.

"Go over to the MacDonald Hotel right away for an interview with Charlotte Whitton," he said. "Tommy was to go and he's tied up at City Hall. Bill's just called in sick."

"Charlotte who?" I asked. But he waved me off. There was no time to do my homework. I grabbed my notebook and galloped.

Miss Whitton was waiting in the lobby with the suggestion that we go up to the mezzanine for tea. I simply didn't know where to begin or what to say, as my first faltering questions made all too clear. Yet instead of expressing some contemptuous sentiments concerning the quality of talent dispatched on a newsworthy story, Miss Whitton carefully put down her teacup and looked at me with warm, womanly understanding. "You haven't been doing this type of assignment long, have you?"

"No," I stuttered miserably. "The man who was supposed to be here . . . . "

"We can do as well as any man," she said firmly. "Now get out your book and pencil. Write carefully and I'll tell you what you are supposed to ask me, and then I'll give you the answers." Patiently, Whitton interviewed Whitton for me.

My story, with its grasp of a new and complex concept, the *modus operandi*, fact and figure, cause and effect, quotes from the prime minister and others, startled MacPherson more than the poem had done. I suspect, as I told the late wonderful woman many times over a long and very dear friendship, that interview really started me on my way. I studied it, took it apart, reassembled it, and I began to see how these things work.

It also meant the beginning of the end of my years at the *Edmonton Journal*. I was ready, not too many moons later, to take a new, more responsible, and better-paid post, in what was going to be an incredible period of my newspaper work, at the *Edmonton Bulletin*.

Gone would be the affectionate paternalism of Charlie Morrison. A close friend of his daughters, I had spent many weekends in their home as one of the family. When I handed in my resignation, he called my father. "What's happening to our daughter, Alex?"

And my father replied, "I guess she has to move along, Charlie, to wherever it is she thinks she's going."

Four

Some great leap forward, you might have said — a young reporter shifting from the evening *Journal* to the morning *Bulletin*.

In the late 1920s the *Journal* was the solidly established, comfortably ensconced publication of the big Canadian Southam chain. The *Bulletin*, although one of the West's oldest papers, had been purchased from its publisher, Frank Oliver, M.P., by a businessman entrepreneur who dabbled in small newspapers, as he did in other investments. His name was Charlie Campbell.

Campbell had offered me what seemed a princely salary in those days — $40 a week when I'd been making $28. Furthermore, I was growing up; I needed new challenge. As if all that weren't enough inducement, there was the *Bulletin* staff. They were more like the dashing, devil-may-care news sleuths I'd read about than were the staid, family-oriented men of the *Journal*.

Along with all the young Canadians at the *Bulletin*, there still were a few holdovers from the "old" *Bulletin* days, like the former publisher's son, Frank Oliver. In 1879 his father had brought the presses for the paper from Winnipeg by Red River cart and across the Saskatchewan River on a raft.

Enlivening the scene was a smattering of unusual characters from Britain and the United States who, for reasons often best known to themselves, had come to light in our small mid-prairie city (around 100,000 at that time). We even had a young English lord, Vivyan by name, who always wore a yellow buttonhole carnation, which frequently froze in below-zero weather. There was also a highly erudite older man who talked like Malcolm Muggeridge until he took me on a walk to White Mud Creek. We resolved that and remained friends.

For well-known Canadian newsmen of later days — like Jim Coleman, Dick Beddoes, Brud Delany, Ray Gardner, Reg Hammond, Dick Jackson, Eric Bland — the *Bulletin* was a great training-ground. In a way, anything went, and life was never dull. Campbell was a friend of William Randolph Hearst and a great admirer of his tabloid-type, muckraking operations. I suspect some of the recruits of my day were dropouts from Hearst newspapers. There were those who had had family and/or drinking problems and had abandoned, or resolved by absention, the former, if not always the latter.

Our managing editor was a charming man and fine writer. His name was Bill de Grave, and its mention in press circles, both then and for many years after, would prompt instant affectionate recounting of marvellous anecdotes. His daily column about current happenings was written in an old English style that would have stood up well in Samuel Pepys's day. Bill's staff was small, his competition large, fat, and self-satisfied, but he could do more to enliven the newsroom and often endless hours of work (there were no newspaper guilds then) than anyone I have known since. He had a joy in life that warmed us all, and some of his escapades were legend.

Earlier, as a reporter in Calgary, Bill and a few of the boys in the city room had once wound up a long night's work with a few drinks and decided to roar around town in a handy red fire engine. Leader-driver Bill was arrested, refused to pay a fine, and went to jail. From that gloomy sepulchre he wrote and somehow managed to smuggle out a daily column so hilarious and so denigrating to the correctional elite and the city fathers that his release was tactfully sought. Finally, with the whole town convulsed, he was forcibly evicted and escorted back to his place of business.

Bill had a good voice, and on occasion in Edmonton he would gather staffers and hangers-on still around after midnight and make his way to the nearby MacDonald Hotel lobby. There, mounting a chair, he would conduct an impromptu sing-song, to the enjoyment of passing travellers and other loiterers who found the scheduled night life of the city less than stimulating at the time.

I have often quoted Bill's remarks to a delegation of angry women who came to protest the reporting of a vice clean-up featured night after night on the *Bulletin*'s front pages. Such lurid investigative reportage tended to occur at periods coincidental with declines in never-healthy circulation sufficient to concern advertisers.

"Mr. Editor," began the middle-aged leader of the troops, a feather in her hat twitching to punctuate her words. "This newspaper is coming into decent homes, and children are reading it. This . . . this . . .white slave thing isn't fit for family consumption. That last part of the story yesterday, and the one the day before, down there where you give the address of the house on _____ Street, were shocking!"

The editor smiled his unruffled, friendly-neighbour smile. "It was good of you to do such painstaking research," he noted. Then he turned his prematurely greying head and the full gaze of blue, innocent eyes on the lady."But, madam, I should hate to think the day would ever come when virtue would be news.''

That remark can still stand up when readers complain that the press is too given to reporting the darker side of life, the sensational, the abnormal. Ah, that's the point. Millions of ordinary people live their lives out doing decent, ordinary things in a non-newsy way. It's the two-headed calf, the miscreant who outrages the normal flow of behaviour, low standards in high places, the effects of a sudden break in ordinary routine caused by fire, flood, famine, murder, or other disaster that make news.

During my days at the *Bulletin*, we also went through the sensational John Brownlee trial. The Alberta Farmer Party premier, a God-fearing family man who did not smoke or drink, was accused of seduction by a young woman. Mrs. Brownlee, a gracious and lovely woman, had been a registered nurse and opened her home for weekend visits to young girls from out of town who were in training. One of them, Vivian McMillan by name, claimed the premier had forced his attentions on her in a guest bedroom.

My paper had strong Liberal Party leanings and was trying editorially to help break the Farmer Party's stranglehold on government. In all fairness, the case made headlines around the English-speaking world, and for years afterwards I would be asked about it. The *Bulletin* did not stint in news coverage.

It was embarrassing to me personally. I wasn't involved as a reporter, but I belonged to a poetry-reading group, all much older women who met at one another's homes. Mrs. Brownlee was one of the most involved members, often entertaining us at her place. (She did not, as so many people do, take out her agonized revulsion for luridly detailed accounts in the newspaper on an individual and non-responsible staffer. When I left Edmonton, her husband's career ruined and her own life shattered, she presented to me, on behalf of the poet-tasters, a beautifully bound volume of Elizabeth Barrett Browning's *Sonnets from the Portuguese*. I still have it.)

I never revealed my own disgust at visits from the "innocent, wronged" young Vivian to the *Bulletin* offices. She approached me one day, as the only woman in the newsroom, with a sheaf of press photographs that had just been taken of her.

"Which do you think is the best of me?" she smirked, as though about to select an illustration for a fashion feature or a beauty contest.

"I'm not a very good judge," I said, ". . . of photographs," and turned back to my typewriter.

Life at the *Bulletin* meant my whole direction had taken a sharp curve windwards. I became a night person, as you do on a morning newspaper, experiencing a camaraderie with my peers you seldom find on an evening sheet. (I still miss this on *The Toronto Star*, where most reporters arrive in early morning and rush home at day's end.) There were all sorts of visiting firemen — syndicate service and other salesmen, late-party attenders, sports figures, politicians, and press agents — who often arrived in a somewhat amorous mood by the time they finished the long train journey from New York, Chicago, or Toronto.

By now I was pantingly compensating for my wallflower years at school. There were lots of beaux to go around, and we danced, skated, went canoeing on the river, had wonderful weekends in Jasper and Banff, and sang around home pianos.

I determined early never to marry a newspaperman, even if one should ask me, despite the natural affinity developed in working together. A couple were foolish enough to do it, too. In those days a woman in the business world usually retired at marriage. Most certainly her presence was no longer permitted when a dear little stranger became a discernible factor in her appearance. (Female teacher friends of mine who married secretly were fired when this disgraceful breach of conduct was discovered.) My philosophy — it probably wouldn't hold a smudge of printer's ink now — was that the good and successful newsmen were going to be away an awful lot, and *I'd* have to stay home and bring up the family. And I didn't want a poor achiever.

Most of us adhered pretty strictly to the accepted morality of the period: wedding band before bed. Of course, there was no pill then, and I am not prepared to argue the virtue of either old or new morality.

So much for sex at the time. I was on a giant ferris wheel. On the down swoops I'd think of a husband and children and find myself getting engaged. Then would come the swing to the top, and a view of a whole great unexplored world out there.

By now my parents had adopted the orphaned son of my mother's brother. He was about seven when the latest of a long line of briefly affianced young men came to ask my father for my hand. As he was leaving the house following congratulations from my parents and their happy acquiescence (they thought it was time their daughter settled down like her friends), the little boy followed him to his car. Out of earshot, he said, "I wouldn't count on Lotta too much if I were you. She hardly ever gets married."

But I did — to a young English accountant with whom I had no more in common than a mutual love of books and theatre. It lasted six months, then I moved back home. He learned at the time what I have learned since: I was too spoiled, too immature for serious dedication to a marriage. A newspaper was deadly competition for my affections. When I could not learn to attend to both husband and job, the job would win. Later, at last grown up, I was able to make a successful marriage that lasted for thirty years, until my husband's death.

By now, I was covering events and stories as far away as Vancouver and Winnipeg. I had safaried into the great Peace River country, visiting the Alberta ranch of the then Prince of Wales. I'd toured Indian reserves and Mennonite settlements and interviewed trappers, traders, university professors, and people in the new labour movement — and, of course, visiting celebrities (such as came our way), including the then prime minister of Canada, Richard B. Bennett.

It was time to broaden horizons. I had been saving pennies, even quarters and dollars, and approached Mr. Campbell one day about taking a six-week journalism course at Columbia University in New York. There are many fine courses in Canada now, but there were none then. If the publisher would give me leave of absence without pay, I'd come back a greater asset, etc.

He tapped a well-manicured hand on his mahogany desk and said curtly, "I've no use for journalism courses. They're a lot of nonsense."

Crushed, I turned to go. Then he added, "But I'll pay your salary and expenses for a six-week 'course' with some of the editors and reporters I know on a few American newspapers with real guts. I'll write ahead and arrange everything."

Columbia could wait. (I never got there.)

I went, as arranged, to the Seattle *Post Intelligencer*, Portland *Oregonian*, San Francisco *News*, and Los Angeles *Herald Examiner*. I even wheedled an extra lovely two weeks out of the publisher for Hollywood, a first of many visits there. All this provided learning experience — indeed, much more comprehensive than my benefactor, in his admiration for men of the ilk of William Randolph Hearst, would have anticipated. Especially helpful were the staffers who worked in such empires. San Francisco was the hottest newspaper town, and I went on assignments with a top and tough little woman reporter who enthralled me with tales of her lovers. She took me on an interview with an accused murderer's wife; to a mysterious many-layered and bunked Chinatown opium den; to watch the widow of the late escape artist Houdini wait for communication from her dead husband.

It was all exciting — the *Bulletin* philosophy blown to giant size. In Hollywood, I passed up the chance to interview a young German actress who had just arrived, Marlene Dietrich, although I've had that debatable pleasure since. The same day had offered opportunity to visit Pickfair, the great mansion of Mary Pickford and Douglas Fairbanks. One day I saw young Douglas Fairbanks, Jr., whiz through a studio lot on a motorcycle, stopping to kiss a slim, young, freckle-faced girl named Joan Crawford, who was his wife. The studio "executive" who offered a film role in return for certain rather indelicately outlined instant favours turned out to be a prop man on the Rin Tin Tin dog series. My rejection was as scornful as it had been when, a small child, I was stopped by a scruffy, unshaven man and offered candy if I'd go with him to the wooded corner lot to pick flowers. "Ho!" I said. "Go yourself. My daddy owns a candy shop."

I came home to Edmonton aglow with adventure and determined to repay the boss with good performance — then to take off to farther fields. But something had happened while I was on the train journey back. The date was October 24, 1929. The stock market had crashed. Depression was upon us — it was as simple as that.

Staffers on my paper, as elsewhere, were fired right and left. I was lucky to be retained, with a salary cut back to $28 a week. I worked, not with all the glamorous new-found ideas of the "course" but at making up pages, writing heads, even doing promotion and a shopping column that would bring in a few advertising dollars.

My father lost his business and, mortgaging the house in an attempt to save it, lost that. The carriage trade we so carefully nurtured had continued to run up bills at the Bon Ton, then shopped for cash at burgeoning chain-store groceterias.

Good, hard-working men were out of jobs, homes, eating money . . . but not of pride. Everyone was stunned. My family was able to get three rooms over a tailoring shop near where the Bon Ton had been. In lieu of rent, my parents

Lotta with Murray Matheson and Marlene Dietrich, whom she finally interviewed in 1960.

cleaned up the shop. There was running water but no bathroom. We used the public toilet downstairs, took sponge baths, or frequented the nearby YWCA and YMCA. For a period we managed on my salary; during the great Depression, a lot of young people heaved to in that manner.

The young, not so seared by loss of dignity or possession, managed to enjoy life and forged a lot of new values, which many of us hold to this day. I spent most of my waking time at the *Bulletin* and weekends with girl friends, a number of whom had married.

As often happens in times of trouble, it was my gentle, protected mother who became the strength of the family. A wonderful cook, she had been a generous donor of good baking to local bazaars, church and lodge groups, and other charities. Drugstores were just beginning to put in tables and serve snacks, and so one night my mother walked to the corner drugstore with a basket of her special devil's food cake and peanut butter cookies. It was a brave thing to do, for she was timid. She presented her wares, offering to provide more if they were acceptable. They were, most definitely. Her reputation had preceded her.

Meanwhile, my father had begun selling vacuum cleaners from door to door and, incidentally, became one of the star salesmen for Electrolux. Sometimes I went with him on "demonstrations" when he felt it would help to have a reporter as a back-up. I've seen my father sell these machines in houses where there wasn't a rug on the floor. He had a way.

By the time the Depression eased and my parents were able to buy a small house in the west end, my mother could have had a factory and staff. Her clients had far surpassed her ability to supply, despite her long hours, day- after- day. But she was a wise woman. She had filled the breach, but the need was past. My father had always taken care of his family, and she knew how important this was to him. So she quietly settled into her new little home and began growing

31

asters as though there had been no disruption. Why asters, I'll never know. My mother loved asters.

Meanwhile, brighter days appeared at the *Bulletin*. There was a summons from Mr. Campbell.

"You've worked very hard over a difficult period, and I appreciate it," he said. "I'm going to give you a raise and a bonus." Spread on his desk were five crisp, new $100 bills. That was a lot of money. I put my hands behind my back.

"If you give me those, Mr. Campbell, I'll be off to Toronto as soon as I can get a pass." (Those were the days of press passes on railways.)

The plot had been building, but I needed funds. From the Calgary *Herald*, two girl friends of mine had taken the plunge and gone to Toronto. One was the women's editor, Jeannie Alexander, the other the managing editor's secretary, Mahon Card. (They'd probably formed a warm friendship to and from the Ladies' on the floor above or below the city room.) They had found work, rented an apartment, and were pressing me to come. Then Byrne Hope Sanders, editor of *Chatelaine*, for which I had done some freelancing, visited Edmonton. She felt that in three months' time there was every possibility she could hire me as assistant editor. Tommy Wheeler, editor of the Toronto *Star Weekly*, had also bought some of my pieces — another contact. Then a furniture manufacturer from Stratford, Ontario, whose daughter had married my cousin, came to dinner at our house on his way to the west coast on a business trip. He and his wife, he said, would put me up until I got settled . . . in Stratford.

All this passed through my mind. Mr. Campbell reached out and shook hands. "Go ahead," he said, "and if it doesn't pan out, come back." Thus assured, I left home.

Many years later I learned from a source close to national Liberal party mandarins that about the time the *Bulletin* publisher so generously doled out bonuses (others got them, too), party headquarters had allocated a sizeable sum to the paper to help fight Social Credit in an upcoming election. That was the new funny-money party that had Bay and St. James Street bankers, along with Tories and Grits, scared silly. A Bible-quoting zealot named William Aberhart was using the new power of radio to take a poverty-stricken province by storm. The funds I mentioned were to be used, according to the informant, to counteract the impact, especially in smaller towns and villages, of the Social Credit offer of $25 a month unearned income for everyone. When Aberhart swept into power, some of these same communities failed to cast a single Liberal vote. That certainly smelled like diversion of funds from right and proper channels. So my survival kit, those first weeks in the big city, may well have been a gift from the unsuspecting gods of political warfare.

Five

Toronto, in 1935, may not have seemed the little old New York of Canada to every émigré from the prairies. But for this one, lugging a big battered Underwood (who could afford a portable?) and with upper-berth accommodation on the CNR, it was instant love. That love still lasts.

For years, when I was a child, Toronto had been merely the place where we changed trains on a visit to paternal grandparents in Stratford, Ontario. We never left Union Station. Our other regular trek was to Seattle, Washington, where my American-born mother's parents lived. It would have seemed foolish to my father to travel anywhere outside Alberta except to spend time with relatives or friends.

Europe, Africa, and Asia were concepts as remote as the moon and as mysterious, except by word-of-missionary. Once in Vancouver, about to take the night-boat to Seattle, Dad scooped up a handful of sea water, tasted it, then gazed far out over the briny. "Now, what would the Lord have had in mind, creating all that water you can't even drink, do you think?'' It was the closest I ever heard him come to criticism of his Maker.

He couldn't understand anyone leaving Edmonton voluntarily, a puzzlement still prevalent among the citizenry there. On a recent visit there, my son mentioned to several people that his mother had been born and had grown up in the Alberta capital. Oftener than not, he was asked, sympathetically, ''What happened to her?''

But now my parents, in company with a group of friends and fellow workers, were at the train wishing me luck in my new venture. Edmontonians are great see-ers off-ers, and it was a relief to be able to enjoy this heart-warming expression of good will at last. ''At last'' because for many years the practice was verboten on our trips to Vancouver en route to Seattle. The CNR commissary man for that run ordered supplies from the Bon Ton, and usually the whole dining-car crew came to our house for a meal on stop-overs. They brought such gifts as great jars of creamy tomato soup and crisp little pillow-shaped biscuits. In return for our hospitality, my parents and I were their ''guests'' when travelling to the west coast. It was necessary to lounge unobtrusively in the parlour car until the train was out of the station and clear of any snooping inspectors. Then we would be escorted to a beautiful drawing-room with bathroom facilities, there to live a sybaritic life on wheels. That included the best service and meals, breakfast in bed for the lady, and mid-morning and mid-afternoon snacks in the dining-car for the young Dempsey, while my father played cribbage with other buffs in the crew. All gratis by unwitting courtesy of the railway company.

But it was 1935, the Bon Ton was no more, and I was on my own. Farewells over, passengers began to chat as the train got underway. (It's true that Westerners are much friendlier to strangers. I journeyed once with an eastern-born and -bred matron who failed to return the customary wave of a little trackside group to rear-car platform observers. The train was passing a lonely whistle-stop in the Rockies. "But I don't know them," she pointed out and had to be informed that hereabouts this was an accepted custom that threatened no further involvement.)

It was quite okay for a young lady to accept dinner invitations from fellow train travellers, most of whom were men travelling on business. Thus along with a senator from home and the president of the University of Alberta, who provided sustenance and avuncular advice, I met a gentle, rather shy young Torontonian named Albert.

Albert (not his real name — he still may be around somewhere) was a scion of one of Ontario's oldest and most prominent families. He took me dancing at the King Edward Hotel the night of our arrival and soon became a frequent visitor to our apartment, an agreeable spare man or escort to females from out of town. He helped make sandwiches for parties, stayed to wash dishes, and was a kind of all-purpose friend of the family. He never made passes or seemed to favour one or the other of the three girls in residence.

You can imagine our shock, then, when Jeannie brought home a copy of *Hush*, the scandal sheet of the day. There on the front page was a picture of our self-effacing Albert. He'd been named as co-respondent in a juicy divorce case. The object of his affection was the beautiful and sexy wife of the scion of another very old Toronto family. We all wondered if she, too, were of United Empire Loyalist stock, mention of which was one of the few vanities Albert allowed himself. If we were serving as cover, Albert paid in good coin, and we missed him. We never heard from him after that day.

I had expected a somewhat humble habitat, probably in a respectable rooming house, for three virtuous and impecunious young ladies far from home. To the contrary. My friends from Calgary had rented sizeable quarters in one of the few fine mid-town apartments then in the city, the Queen's Park at 89 Breadalbane Street, long since razed. Our place was kitty-corner to the legislative buildings, with beautiful Queen's Park at our front door. Here were lush grassy walks, masses of flowers, and big trees — a favourite strollery, especially on misty spring nights with a male companion. One of mine, at such a season, brought along a sturdy umbrella and was highly adept at hooking down masses of horse-chestnut blossoms for our flower vases. That's the one I married, naturally. Many years later it was not surprising that his son should appear with a strangely reminiscent gift when, with a whole cub troop in tow, he arrived to visit me in hospital and share joy over a new baby brother. They came on a day in May, my eight-year-old bearing armloads of flowering crabapple, lilac, and spiraea, though we had none such on our property. Did I speak of cub's honour? Certainly not. The intent was to delight, though deed be dark as night. And you can't argue with genes.

Looking over the tenants' name plates one day I noticed Michener, Mr. and Mrs. Roland. Jeannie knew who they were, of course. She always knew who everybody was. "A nice young couple. He's a lawyer, and they've moved here from Alberta." Michener later was to become Speaker of the House of Commons, Canadian High Commissioner to India, and Governor-General of Canada.

Many of the other tenants were equally as interesting, in other ways. As mentioned, we were steps from the legislative buildings. One of my escorts had boasted of knowing a then prominent cabinet minister. In the elevator one day I recognized this gentleman from his many press pictures and nudged my companion. I got a quick kick in the ankle. After the passenger had departed, I snorted. "Ha! So you know the honourable so-and-so!"

"Yes, I do," he said sharply, "but some of the politicians have lady . . . ah . . . friends living here, and it is understood one does not press acquaintance if one sees them in the vicinity."

True or false, I can't attest. Anyone can be under suspicion, as I realized one Sunday morning when I was leaving our apartment to go to church. Four . . . count them . . . four pairs of big men's overshoes forgotten by guests after a Saturday night party were lined neatly in the corridor outside our door.

It was at this time that I made my first motor trip to Niagara Falls, a highly anticipated treat. When I awoke and found it was raining, I turned over in bed. The friend who was taking us called to see if we were ready.

"But we won't be going in the rain, will we?" I asked. Of course, we would, she said. It would probably clear, and this was just a light shower anyway. When she arrived, she looked at my scarf-tied head, heavy old tattered raincoat, and high rubber boots. I had a worn sweater and skirt underneath.

"Where's the hard-times party?" she asked. "I thought we were going to the Brock (an elegant hostelry much favoured by honeymooners) for lunch."

I explained I had an overnight bag with a good dress and shoes. But in case we got stuck in the mud, I was an expert at car-pushing. She looked at me to see if I was serious.

"The highway from Toronto is paved," she said. And I replied with words that became a slogan around our apartment for my many future small-town misconceptions:

"All the way to Niagara Falls?"

Our apartment overflowed with people. We had arrived on a wave of ambitious young seekers after wider and more lucrative opportunity, from the prairies and the Maritimes. In a smaller way, they were giving staid old T'ranna a shot in the arm, as later swarms of Europeans were to do on a grand scale.

It was the best of all times and the best of all places, in our minds. We were young, full of *joie de vivre*, wonder, and the energy to work all day and dance the nights away. (Ah, Horace Lapp at the Royal York, the King Eddie's

Romanelli, whoever was at the Old Mill.) Inevitably, of course, we three would marry and go our separate, if deeply affectionate, ways. But all young women should have some such magic interlude, clear of parental control, before taking on the responsibilities of their own families. We had the stabilizing influence of such older people as those we met through the Canadian Women's Press Club. Jeannie and I had both been officers of our small branches in the west and found generous and big-sisterly warmth in the Toronto club.

You learn a lot of give-and-take, sharing an apartment with other girls. At home my mother always laid my clothes out for a party and kept them laundered and mended. For weeks in Toronto I was saying, "I'm sorry," for my inadvertent sins of omission—leaving clothes scattered about, burning a meal, forgetting my turn to do something. I was better prepared for marriage the second time around.

Our greatest pals, apart from boy friends, were a foursome of young men who had come to 89 Breadalbane from Hamilton. Having missed brothers in my own life, I found this an especially wonderful relationship. It may seem strange, but none of us "went out" with each other. We were borrowers and lenders from one apartment to the other and formed a habit of often having Sunday breakfast together, when we laughed our way through accounts of Saturday night dates and adventures elsewhere.

When someone telephoned, "Soup's on," we foregathered as we were, which usually meant pyjamas and dressing-gowns. Since we wore flannelette or heavy cotton and my dressing-gown at that time was a long, faded purple chenille number with high buttons, our attire was hardly conducive to orgy.

After breakfast, we three would either leave, if guests, or shoo out the boys, if hosts, and get neatly clothed and hatted for morning service at Eaton Memorial Church. We were not compulsive worshippers, I am afraid, so much as recipients of the hospitality of a lovely old couple we discovered there,

39

who usually took two or three young people in the congregation home to Sunday dinner. They lived nearby, and Mrs. R. did roast beef and butterscotch pie with a divinity befitting the Sabbath. It was not difficult to appear forlorn and in need of mothering. Usually we had been partying very late the night before.

One Sunday morning when the boys were breakfast hosts, there was a shortage of butter. I offered to go down to our apartment for some. As I was taking it out of the refrigerator, a knock sounded at the door — it was the Stratford furniture manufacturer and his wife, the ones who had offered to give me refuge until I got settled in the East. Mr. Strudley was going west again and wanted to be able to take news of my welfare to my family. Then the telephone rang. It was John from upstairs.

"Did you go back to bed?" he wanted to know. "Where's the butter?"

"Yes," I said. "I mean no. I'll deliver that parcel to you after church. I'm tied up now."

I could hear him whistle and turn to the others. "I told you that crazy, poetry-scribbling girl would crack up. It's happened. I'd better go right down." There was a click before I could say anything else.

Sure enough, a heavy pounding soon rattled the door. I continued to talk to the Strudleys. Mrs. S. looked alarmed. "Aren't you going to answer?"

"It's probably the wrong number — I mean, wrong apartment. We get a lot of that here."

"Well, we'll soon find out," Mr. Strudley said and opened to the sight of a handsome but tousled, dark-haired young man in pyjamas and dressing-gown.

He was also a very bright young man. Taking in the situation at a flash, John mumbled, "Oh, I'm sorry, I must have gotten off at the wrong floor."

"Well, keep your wits about you next time," said the older man. "Yes, sir," John said, and disappeared.

That morning the company of good companions, minus one, ate dry toast. I sent the Strudleys happily off to Edmonton with an excellent report. At Christmas, I opened a big gift-wrapped box and found a pair of silk pyjamas and a pretty dressing-gown. The card read, "From all of us. Now, can we burn the purple bath robe?" It had six signatures.

Not too long ago I ran into another grandmother at a very proper dinner party, and we discovered we had both lived on Breadalbane Street. Now, something that had always puzzled our threesome was where and how the boys found firewood whenever we needed it for our open grates. Nobody could spare money for that kind of thing, and a couple of them would fill our basket when they did theirs. The wood was strangely jagged, rough and in chunks, often varnished and with nails sticking out. The boys explained that they knew a wrecker tearing down some old houses and he was glad to have the stuff carried away.

My *vis-à-vis* at dinner said across the table, "You know, we lived in one of the nice old houses near the corner. But there was one period when we had a terrible time with vandals. They would keep prying pieces off our doorsteps. No one ever could catch them at it, and they must have come from a distance. It was such a nice neighbourhood, with just the nuns in the high-walled convent across the way. And, of course, that lovely apartment building."

Six

For someone who's grown up knowing everyone in a small city, there's a special kind of aloneness walking the concrete canyons of a strange big one — especially if you're wondering where you're going to find work. To this day, I recognize it with great empathy — those people confused by the hustle and bustle, the uncaring street crowds, the clipped impersonality of officials and attendants.

First, I thought, I'll try the Toronto *Star Weekly*. I'd had some correspondence with the editor, Tommy Wheeler, and he had used some pieces of mine.

He was the kindest of men. I explained my expectations — or hope — of a job on *Chatelaine* within a few weeks. Byrne Hope Sanders had indicated that I might fill the role of assistant editor. But I knew I would have to pass *her* boss at the big publishing complex — *Maclean's* — of which the women's magazine was a part. Wheeler offered temporary asylum, with a desk and assignments, on a free-lance basis. Then we'd see what happened.

I knew who the man at the next desk was, of course. Gregory Clark, along with artist Jimmy Freise, did a weekly humorous feature that was as familiar to Canadians everywhere as the work of Ann Landers or Pierre Berton today. Or Gregory Clark. Greg wrote, as he does now, with a clarity, gentle wit, and seeming ease, which is what greatness is all about.

Timidly, I introduced myself, and he looked at me with keen, friendly eyes.

"Lotta. A lovely name. Like Lotte Lehmann."

Stunned at anyone thinking such a name nice, I asked, "Who is Lotte Lehmann, Mr. Clark?" He explained that she was the great lieder singer and also the finest soprano of the day at the Metropolitan Opera House in New York.

I blushed. "You must think me very ignorant."

He patted my hand. "No. Just unaware. You'll soon learn." Then he added slowly, "You're just beginning here. May I suggest something? No matter what anybody asks you to do or be, don't try to be anything else but Lotta Dempsey. I've always just been Greg Clark. Nobody else wants to, or can, be Greg Clark or Lotta Dempsey."

As I came to know Greg better, I gathered my quota of stories about him, as all his friends have done. My favourite is a happening of not too long ago. At the age of 82, with his treasured wife gone, Greg has lived for some time in the downtown King Edward Hotel. As he was walking slowly back from Eaton's big Queen Street department store one day, a couple standing on a corner observed his progress. Every few steps he would stop and speak to someone. When he approached the pair, the man reached into his pocket and took out two one-dollar bills.

"Here, dad," he said, sympathetically. "We're American visitors and you look like too nice an old man to have to stop so many people for a hand-out."

Greg pulled up to his full five foot two, settled a battered fedora a bit more firmly on his white head, and snorted, "I'll have you know those people were stopping *me*. I wasn't stopping *them*. They recognized me and wanted to say hello."

"Oh," said his would-be benefactor. "Sorry. You must be some kind of character around here."

Canada's most revered elder fourth-estatesman walked on to the hotel. He reported later to his great friend, *The Globe and Mail* columnist Bruce West, "I looked at myself in the rotunda mirror, and I thought, some kind of character, am I? Why didn't I tell them I was a writer and not unknown?" But it was too late.

Tom Wheeler's assistant, Gwen Cowley, passed along my first assignment. It was to make a selection of private secretaries of top Torontonians in different fields and interview them about their jobs and bosses.

"Great!" I said enthusiastically. "I'll start right away." I walked out into a corridor and stood there, helpless. I didn't know any heads of anything in Toronto. Where to begin? A nice-looking young man, tell-tale sheaf of copy paper in hand, came by.

"Are you a *Star* reporter?" I asked. He nodded. It was Frank Chamberlain, one of the paper's best by-liners. I presented my dilemma. Newsmen around the globe, as I have confirmed many times at home and abroad, are the most helpful people in the world to others in their trade (apart from the immediate opposition, of course). Frank sat down with me and listed a half-dozen names, telephone numbers, and addresses.

There was one secretary-and-boss team whose story did not appear in that first on-location piece I was to write in Toronto. He was among the city's best-known men, later to become a national figure. The day of our appointment turned out to be an unfortunate one. I followed a pattern I had worked out of first interviewing the executive about his secretary, then the woman about her boss. Apparently unconscious of the troubled state of his employee at the time, the gentleman gave a glowing account of her value and virtues. He introduced us, then left for an appointment elsewhere.

She was a vivid little redhead and, like so many of us in emotional crisis, found a stranger's shoulder comfortable to cry on.

"Do you do special things for Mr. B., like remind him of his wife's birthday, remember where he put his overshoes, stuff like that?" I asked innocently.

The dam burst. "You can say I'm going to tell him to take his overshoes out from under my bed," she said, bitterly. "So he says I'm a good secretary! Well I'm not good and (honest to Pete, she used these familiar words) I've been a lot more than a secretary to him!"

I left quietly, scratching the names off my list. Furthermore, I never heard from Mr. B., as one so often does if an interview fails to appear in its appointed place. When I married and came to know a great number of Torontonians through my husband and his family, I met the B's many times and was invited to their home. I often looked at him quizzically but there was never a gleam of recognition. There are a number of things in this world, along with sleeping dogs, it is best to let lie.

Another incident comes to mind. At one time my husband and I and our children were living in an upper duplex at a corner with a sharp turn where motor accidents were not infrequent. One night we heard a screech of wheels and a great crash; we looked out to see a car over the sidewalk and accordioned against a brick wall.

My husband ran down and soon came back with a man, unhurt, and a pretty woman streaming blood. We administered first aid, found the cuts superficial, called a cab, and they went on their way with profuse thanks.

Some weeks later, there was a knock at the door. We had been expecting friends, and both went to answer. To our surprise, it was the man of the car accident, with a quite different and far from attractive woman. He looked my husband straight in the eye, with an age-old plea for male collusion.

"I must beg your pardon for this really unpardonable intrusion," he said, "but my wife insisted on my bringing her here. Will you please confirm that I was alone the night my car crashed into your corner?"

He had not expected the added hazard of a woman to be won to the conspiracy. Before my husband spoke, I said, "Of course you were alone, Mr. _____. Have there been some later effects from the shaking up?"

"No," he said, looking as grateful as I have ever seen a man. "*It's very kind of you* to be concerned."

I did feel a little ashamed at the woman's profuse apologies. "I feel such a fool," she said, putting an arm around her husband. "Please forgive me."

As I say, lying is not just for sleeping dogs. In some situations, it has its place.

As it evolved, I was not to be at the *Star Weekly* for long. Less than three weeks after I arrived in Toronto, the appointment as assistant editor of *Chatelaine* came through. The Maclean Publishing Company was by far Canada's biggest publisher of consumer magazines and technical and business periodicals. Its leading consumer publication was, of course, *Maclean's*. *Chatelaine*, the women's magazine, was relatively new. The late Napier Moore, one of the country's wittiest speakers and a discerning editor, was editorial director of *Chatelaine*, as well as boss man at *Maclean's*.

Byrne Sanders was an able editor, an enthusiast (I don't like negative people), and an excellent teacher. Our budget was limited, our staff very small, and at one time I was writing under four names: Lotta Dempsey, Carolyn Damon (fashions), Annabel Lee (beauty), and John Alexander (features). It was great fun, at long last, to choose names I liked.

Time came when I thought I was away to the races, and

Byrne felt she could leave me to go off on some speaking and other editorial engagements. On one occasion I had put the magazine to bed in her absence, having written several pieces for the issue. A proof copy had just arrived when I was summoned to the sanctum of Napier Moore. He was not a patient man, and his sarcasm could sting.

He leaned back in his chair. I shivered nervously. His scowl was foreboding as he handed me the magazine.

There was a large circle in red ink around a sentence in one of my articles. I had used the word "we". Today, with so much personalized journalism, so many by-lines, "we" and "I" are often acceptable from the writer. They were not then.

After a stern reprimand, Mr. Moore said, "The only writers permitted use of the word 'we' around here are editorial writers and people with tapeworms."

Indelible. The next thing he had to say stayed with me, too. We had printed rejection slips on blue paper that were attached to articles when returned to writers not sufficiently talented or important to rate a personal letter. I had returned an article by one of Canada's most distinguished writers (the fact that I hadn't heard of him was no excuse) with a printed slip. The letter he then wrote to Napier Moore was scathing. What kind of ignoramuses was *Maclean's* employing these days? Who had dared to perpetrate this indignity?

Confronted with this missive, I was near tears. "I'll never do it again, Mr. Moore. I promise. Never, never."

The editor was softening a little. He had inflicted a justifiable wound. He smiled. "Like sleeping with another man's wife, Lotta. Once is too often."

On the whole, though, things were very good, and once back under Byrne's protective shadow, I enjoyed both my job and my leisure. I was moving around — we were, after all, a national magazine — doing stories in Quebec and through Ontario. In Ottawa, I was again to meet Prime Minister R. B. Bennett and to talk with his successor, Prime Minister Mackenzie King.

Working on a monthly magazine allowed some relief from the unending demands of the daily deadline and the opportunity for more in-depth research and writing than I had been involved in heretofore. So I had a full week to take notes on the Dominion Drama Festival in Ottawa.

The next year, 1936, was another turning point for me. That's when I married a young architect with two young sons. In a divorce, he had won custody of his children and lived with them and a housekeeper in a pleasant house in a nice part of town. When I met and fell in love with Dick, once again my life took a swift curve in direction.

This was my first involvement with the bright young intellectuals who had come out of university ready to contribute to a world that had no place for them. Largely, they were children of professional people, some wealthy, others not. They belonged to fraternities and sororities. They took university for granted as much as my lower middle-class upbringing had taken high school. It was an experience for me. The world of the press was one thing. But I had been accustomed to men and women whose private pursuits were strictly segregated. At parties, for example, the men played cards; women sewed, gossiped, and prepared food. Even the younger people, especially the boys, had little opportunity for immersion in books, music, ballet, opera, or symphony. Suddenly, here was a world for which I had been waiting and hoping. I loved it, despite some rude shocks due to my somewhat prudish and limited upbringing.

On my first date with my future husband, he took me to a symphony with Reginald Stewart conducting at Varsity Stadium. These were wonderful summer musicfests, and the audience walked around the lovely park-like grounds at intermission.

This man was a new breed to me. He didn't think such entertainment was only for girls and old ladies. Yet he had been middleweight boxing champion at the University of

Toronto and had won a second T in the rowing team. But I was dismayed when he turned up with scuffy sandals, an open-neck shirt, and old bags and blazer. He was a human being who was very comfortable in his skin and could, I learned later, be as elegant as anyone in white tie and tails (admittedly ones inherited from his father) and a tall silk hat at the Royal Winter Fair. (He always called it the mink-and-manure crowd.)

That night during intermission, this strange young man (I had met him through young friends, knew nothing of his background then) shocked me beyond measure. He unwound himself from our balcony bench and excused himself with, "I had beer earlier. I have to go to the john. Right back."

In Edmonton, we did not mention such things. Even at the newspaper office. It seems incredible now, but it's true. So right then I made up my mind that that was the first and last time I would have anything to do with such a crude and ill-mannered fellow.

Dick returned, whistling, took my arm, and started to propel me around the outdoors on a beautiful moonlit night. As I prepared the words to tell him off when he delivered me home, he waved to three charming, typically upper-middle-class Toronto ladies, also strolling. They were in the summer garb of so many older women of their time — white dresses, soft sweaters over their shoulders, white gloves, and tiny strings of pearls.

He pulled me over. "This is my mother and my aunt Grace and aunt Belle. Mother, I would like you to meet Lotta Dempsey."

They were utterly charming, dignified, lovely — the kind of women I had dreamed of becoming. There followed an animated discussion among them — I could only stand by, unable to contribute — about the quality of the French horns, the third movement, the cadenza. They talked thus as my parents discussed movies or cooking or lodge (my father was an Oddfellow, a Mason, and a Shriner; my mother was a Rebekah).

So I decided that here was a conundrum I was not yet capable of solving. I would give it time.

Seven

Some people are born with silver spoons. Others depart the womb disaster-prone.

My gift from whatever spirits hover over new babies was an invisible banana peel, with a lifetime guarantee. I come . . . I see . . . I fall flat on my face in so many different ways and places there's often not a dry eye in the house. Change of scenery makes no matter. I bomb as readily in Guyana as in London, in Inuvik as Sacramento, at sea, on land, or in the air. This behaviour pattern has been unwavering throughout all my years as a reporter, editor, columnist, radio commentator, or television interviewer.

My husband soon became aware of his bride's mental double vision and accepted it with patience and affability, developing a precognition that sometimes, not always, saved the day. When he was not there — and I travelled a great deal alone or with a reporting team on assignments of varying kinds — nature took its stumblebum course.

There was the time, en route to New York on a *Globe and Mail* assignment, that I set an American Airlines plane afire. This doesn't sound like the four-star laugh-in of the season, and provided some very scary moments indeed. As my husband was seeing me off, Johnny Wayne (of Wayne and Shuster) rushed in with an American comedian he had brought to the airport and introduced us. We boarded together. Johnny and Dick went back home.

There was some confusion coming aboard, with a number of small children to be placed, and the stewardess asked me to roll my raincoat under my seat (we were in the front of the economy section) — she'd get it later. I was in the window seat. The performer was very amusing and interesting, and we chatted until we hit rough weather. With the "no smoking" sign lit, I butted my cigarette. I *think* I butted it. I still believe it was one from the ashtray behind mine . . . but no matter. Next thing we knew someone shouted, "Fire!" and , indeed, flame, not just smoke, was shooting up from behind me. We were herded into the aisle as an officer with a fire extinguisher brought the blaze under control. It was my coat.

All I could think of in those few terrifying moments was that I'd have to pay for the plane if it burned, and it must have cost millions. The point that none of us might land for such an assessment didn't occur to me. My name and address were taken, and for weeks afterwards I lived in fear of the postman, but I never heard further from American Airlines.

Completely shaken, I taxied to the Algonquin Hotel, our favourite in Manhattan, checked in, and examined the coat, which I had bundled up and was carrying. It was oozily shredded around great charred gaps, obviously ruined. My husband was to join me the next day, and I certainly didn't want him to know anything about this unless, or until, I needed support. So I put the remains in the wastebasket. I never was very bright. An outdoor trashcan would have been the obvious disposal unit.

Dick was just settling in next day and I was surprising him with the news that I had finally decided to give up smoking when there was a knock at the door. There stood a stern-faced assistant manager, a white carnation in his buttonhole, a lacerated garment in his hand.

"Is this yours, madam?" he asked.

I shook my head. "I never saw it before in my life." (I had an idea the airlines might have sent him, and a posse waited in the corridor to escort me to the penitentiary.)

"Then," said the staff man, stepping in firmly, "We certainly would like to know whose it is, and where the owner is. It was found . . . ."

My husband broke in, looking at me with amazement. "Of course that's my wife's coat. You know perfectly well it is, Lotie. What's the matter with you?" He turned angrily to the hotel man. "And if that's what your cleaning people have done to my wife's coat, you're sure as hell going to pay for it."

So the whole story was tearfully revealed, and I melted into comforting arms. He was shaken, but never mentioned it again. That afternoon he brought me a lovely new raincoat.

Could they but meet, there would be a sizeable fraternity of baffled strangers who have been exposed to my idiocies. One, most certainly, is the gentleman I ran into, naked (me, not him) in a corridor of a posh hotel in Chicago.

I must explain first that I am one of the world's most dedicated train buffs, although I've been required to take all sorts of aircraft, for a number of reasons, from time to time. (I was second female in the world, after an intrepid Briton, to ride in an experimental military jet at Douglas Aircraft in Los Angeles.) But it is well known around the fast-moving, high-speed operation of *The Toronto Star* that I will con the company into a train trip any time possible. I'm enormously cunning about this, for reaction to requests that I take the rails to Vancouver or Halifax or California is tantamount, in this sound-barrier-breaking atmosphere, to suggesting we hitch old Dobbin to the shay. But if it's not a spot news assignment, I point out that a bedroom or roomette on the train will give me ample opportunity to write three or four pieces by the time I get home. Anyway, they humour me when possible.

The hotel incident was on one of many train journeys to Hollywood, Las Vegas, and other dream and nightmare capitals. It was necessary to make a train connection in Chicago after an overnight ride from Toronto, and usually there was a four- to five-hour wait there. So my custom was to have a reservation at a Chicago hotel, freshen up for the days ahead, and perhaps do some work. On this occasion, there was a mix-up about the room, and the desk clerk asked me, apologetically, if I would mind using the presidential suite? I would be there only a few hours, and they'd make the rate as for a single room.

This had to be the most enormous complex of bedrooms, reception room, living-room, dining-room, and bathrooms I had ever seen. Immediately I drew a bath, disrobed in one of the bedrooms, had a long refreshing soak, a brisk dry-off, and started back to the door I thought led to the bedroom and my clothes.

But when I got through, it turned out to be one to the outside corridor. I was understandably confused, and before I realized what had happened, the door swung shut and locked. Just then, around the corner came a very well-dressed man followed by a bellhop with his luggage. Turning my back I called in panic, "I was looking for the bedroom where I left my clothes."

Here was a gentleman indeed, or perhaps he, too, had an idiot wife. Quickly he took off his coat and handed it to the bellhop, who dropped the bags and, without a word, covered me. When he had opened the door with a master key, I passed back the coat, also without a word. God knows what repercussion this might have had upon the reputation of

Franklin Delano Roosevelt, for whom the presidential suite was usually reserved. Bellhops, of course, see many weird things in their day-to-night operations. But the gentleman well might have joined forces with a man on the train, same trip, coming home.

I was really slugging it out with all the notes I had. As insurance for my next jaunt, I planned to write as many pieces as possible on the three-day trip. This time I had a roomette, the involved mechanics of which it is difficult to explain unless you've been in one. There's a lot of living compressed in a very small space. I found when I got a table put up by the porter (with me already seated) and my portable and notes on it, there was difficulty getting out. Since it was now impossible to use the toilet or get a drink, I evolved a clever system: after climbing up on the table and crouching there, I could open the intricately fastened doors, push the folds apart, and slide down into the corridor outside.

Desiring to make one such safari, I climbed up and got the doors open. There was a man sitting in the open doorway of the roomette across from mine. I realized the train was slowing down, and there was no point in going to the Ladies until it started again. ("Kindly do not flush the toilet when the train is in the station.") So I waited.

Always friendly, I said, "Hi. Nice day." He grabbed his bag and rushed for the end of the coach. It wasn't until he hurried by on the platform with one unbelieving look back that I realized I really should have explained why I was crouched on a table in a roomette.

It took Evelyn Caldwell, an ace Vancouver press woman, to alert me years later to an incident of which I was unconscious and which amused her in the midst of an otherwise tragic situation.

Reporters had gathered from far and near for the Winnipeg flood, a disastrous overflow of the swollen Red River that washed whole streets and some residents away, in May of 1950. On a grey early dawn, we were watching rescue boats come down the river, while mud-caked, sweaty men wearily piled sandbags on the shore in an attempt to hold back the water.

Evelyn reports I was standing intent and involved at river's edge as a whole house floated by, with a man, woman, child, dog, cat, and some chickens clinging to the flat roof. As Evelyn approached, I had pad and pencil in hand and was shouting at the top of my lungs, "And what are your initials, Mr. Jones?" You can see my lessons as a cub reporter stuck. Always get the initials.

Usually in my entanglements, the joke was on me. Once I persuaded an aide to President Johnson to show me the historic Oval Room of the White House, where so many cabinet decisions are made. I had been on a number of assignments in the presidential mansion, but never here. The Johnsons were away from Washington. Once there, I begged to sit in the president's chair for one moment. (I wouldn't want to now.) He stood guard at the door and said, grudgingly, "All right, one moment."

I sank into the leather seat, hands on the broad chair arms, and gazed at the table. There, just under the top and in front of the chair, was a panel of four buttons — red, blue, green, and white. Ah, the awesome surge of potential power! Which would get the Pentagon, the Kremlin, 10 Downing Street, or, indeed, light a fuse to nuclear war that could destroy civilization?

You can imagine the drama, the tension of my story for the paper. Unfortunately, the week it appeared, there was a brief item in the "People" column of *Time* magazine. It reported President Johnson had had four coloured buttons installed in front of his chair in the Oval Room: white for milk; red, coffee; blue, a soft drink; and green, water (to accompany aspirin, no doubt). I would have put my life on the green.

But when the famous British author, J. B. Priestley, came to our house in Toronto to a party, the joke was on him, although I'm sure he doesn't know it to this day. Priestley was over from Britain for the opening of a play he had written, which was to be premiered in Toronto. *The Glass Cage* had been designed for three brilliant Toronto actors, Barbara Chilcott and her brothers, Donald and Murray Davis, whom Priestley had seen perform in London. We were having one of our many parties at an old house we had bought after the war at 83 Woodlawn Avenue West, and Herbert Whittaker, then drama critic for *The Globe and Mail* and a long-time friend, asked if he could bring the famed Briton. Of course, we were delighted, although I was a touch concerned, for only that morning in my *Globe* column, "Person to Person", I had been uncharacteristically critical . . . of Mr. Priestley.

He had been guest speaker at a literary luncheon the day before and was introduced by Toronto's greatly loved chief librarian, Charles Sanderson. Mr. Sanderson, a gentle pundit, spoke of the joy Priestley's *Good Companions* had given him. The writer, apparently in a testy mood, opened his remarks by saying he did wish everybody wouldn't talk about *Good Companions* as though it were the only thing he'd ever done. Indeed, he'd written much better things. It was crushing to Mr. Sanderson, and I was accordingly nasty in my column.

I mentioned this to Herbert, who said, "That's all right. I'll simply introduce you as Mrs. Fisher. You write as Lotta Dempsey, so no connection."

All went as planned, and I think our special guest had a good time. There were a number of charming women there, and I observed that Mr. P. had an appreciative eye. Then came the late hour when half-a-dozen lingerers gathered in our little penthouse bar for a final libation. Now comfortable among new friends, the author turned to me and asked if I had seen the column some beastly woman had written about him in the *Globe* that morning.

There was a silence, and I filled it quickly. "Oh, Dempsey. She's a dreadful old bat. Everyone knows that." He was somewhat jolted by my vehemence, as were my other well-wined and -dined guests.

But he seemed appeased. He turned to Herbie. "Is that the general opinion?"

I was beside him and gave a surreptitious poke. "Well," hedged this kindly man, who hates hurting anyone unless it is essential in the line of critical duty, "she must have felt strongly because usually. . . ."

My husband, thoroughly enjoying himself, broke in. "Nonsense, Herbie. You know what she's like. My feeling is, she's terribly frustrated and the best medicine for her would be a good roll in the hay. It would take out some of the prickles. But what man would want to tackle it?"

What man indeed? Somewhat later that early morning, when the party was over and the last guest had departed, the matter was resolved.

Eight

Which would make the scene first? It was a close race between the baby and the new house. Dick had designed and built one of Toronto's first split-levels where a split-level ought to be, snugged into the topside of a beautiful ravine, at 32 Bennington Heights Drive in Leaside. It was the plan of my dreams, in more ways than one, and the architect vowed never again to sleep with a client. Too many pokes in the middle of the night with, "Oh — and I want shelves in the top floor study for my files. Not just bookselves." Or, "Can you make a big plant box inside the entrance just above the free-hanging stairs, with a hidden light shining on the leaves?" And, "Be sure there's room for double bunks and storage areas in the boys' bedrooms, so they can keep extra blankets and sheets and have friends stay without any fuss." (It was impossible to avoid fuss. On one occasion, with young overnight guests, I absent-mindedly insisted on a neighbour child going to bed, despite his protests. I thought it was just that he wanted to stay up later but discovered my error when an anguished mother came to see why he hadn't returned home when he was supposed to.)

Dick's answer usually was a sleepy, "Okay, baby. Now will you please go to sleep?" (Friends who suggested discreetly I stop my husband from calling a mature, five-foot-nine woman "baby" were promptly put in their places. "Why do you think I married him?" I said. "Nobody ever called me 'baby' before.")

My timing was perfect. I managed to be so pregnant when we moved from Clifton Road that I wasn't allowed to carry as much as a book. The first night all that was unpacked in our bedroom-bathroom-balcony master suite was a big mattress and springs. Moving wasn't as professionalized then as now; friends helped and you took a lot of things yourself. Dick came home with masses of spring flowers, put them in a scrub pail in the middle of the floor, and gathered a few bits of leftover building wood for a fire in the bedroom fireplace. He spoke tenderly of the plaque he had designed and sunk in a steel box in the foundations. It read: "This is the house which I have built for Lotta, my wife, whom I love."

It was a moving night, but one many very pregnant women would recognize. I was too uncomfortable to sleep. (My son is now six foot six and a half and big all over. He started big.) So into this lovely romantic scene I injected words familiar to many a father-to-be. "Darling, I can't sleep."

Dick sighed and, for the zenth time, pulled on some clothes. I donned the tent-like shift designed for such as me in those days, and we got into the car.

It was a fresh May night, air fragrant with bloom in what was still unspoiled countryside. We were close to a lovers' lane overlooking the valley, and so Dick pulled in and parked, turning off the lights as a dozen or more other cars had done. We were sharing the peace of the world around when Dick was alarmed to find me opening the door and lumbering out. I turned back and winked. Quietly I moved in from behind one after another of the four-wheeled love nests and, opening a door, said softly, "That will get you this." My bulk was all too well illuminated in the moonlight. Perhaps it was the way we both laughed when we got home at the startled scrambles and quick igniting of engines that accounted for my going to hospital the next day.

That was St. Michael's, in downtown Toronto, a wonderful Catholic hospital. Serene and gentle ministering sisters moved through the wards in their flowing black habits. (Ah, for those days.) The maternity floor supervising sister was an impressive, big woman with noble features and a special penchant for new mothers and babies. Her habit was of creamy white.

At that time King George VI and Queen Elizabeth, now the Queen Mother, were making what was to be their final tour of Canada and visiting Toronto. It was about the only royal tour here I failed to cover, over a period of thirty years or more. We all listened on the radio to the plummy, breathless purple prose with which announcers of the day described such events. Shortly thereafter Sister Vicentia glided in, wreathed in smiles. She carried a bouquet of tiny white rosebuds, pulled one out, and put it on my bed.

"Her Majesty has been sending bouquets presented to her to patients in hospitals," she said, "and asked that this one especially be distributed to mothers of new babies, in memory of her visit and her own loved little daughters, Lillibet and Margaret Rose." (I pressed my rosebud in one of the books on my bedstand and have the faded, dried petals still.)

One evening, many, many years later, I called a taxi at the *Star*, gathered presents I had for my son on his birthday, and prepared to journey the distance to dinner with him, his wife, and small daughter in the suburbs.

The young cabbie was curt to the point of surliness and began driving at a dangerous speed, swerving in and out of traffic. To slow him down without appearing cross, I said, "Hi, there, could you take it a little easier? I've got some presents here for my son's birthday today, and a couple are breakable."

There was a dull "huh" from the front, then, "It's my birthday today, too, and nobody's giving me any presents." The tone was bitter.

I started to talk, as much to keep him from charging ahead madly as anything, and discovered he was separated, broke, and generally fed up with life. I asked his age. "Why, you're the same age as my son." I said. "Where were you born?"

"Toronto."

Then, "What hospital?"

"St. Michael's."

I said excitedly, "Then your mother and I were there, giving birth to our sons, at the same time. She must have told you . . . ."

He broke in acidly, "She didn't have a chance to tell me anything. She died when I was a baby. My father married again, a woman with kids of her own. I had a rough time. Anyway, you wouldn't have seen my mother. She'd have been in a public ward. We were very poor."

I leaned forward and touched his shoulder. "Would you like to know what it was like the day you were born? My son liked to hear it."

He relaxed a little and nodded. I described the scene, the crowds in the streets because of the royal visit and my concern that the doctor wouldn't make it through the traffic jams. And I told him how Dr. O'Leary, who probably delivered his mother, too, and had a wooden leg, said not to worry, he'd hop through waving it if necessary. By the time I got to the Queen's bouquet of white rosebuds we had arrived at my son's house. The driver pulled to a stop, turned around, and gazed at me with a strange and wondering look in the hard, narrowed eyes I had been watching in the rear-view mirror. He said, very, very softly, "Then that's what the dried-up petals are in my mother's Bible. I always wondered."

With my baby coming, I had resigned happily from the staff of *Chatelaine*, keeping on some departmental work, such as the beauty section. I remember once when I was miserably heavy with child and feeling ill, Dick wrote the column and came to read it to me where I lay in bed. At one point he rhapsodized, "What do you want to be tonight, O lady fair, a flaming hibiscus or a languorous lily? Then take your choice of make-up." He turned to look at his own light of love and noted, sympathetically, "You do look quite green, baby. I'll get you something."

I was to do other assignments, too, and write some for *Maclean's* magazine. Dick had built me a study above the lower floors of the house, with all their hubble and bubble, with its own small fireplace and balcony sheltered in treetops. Lights from the city across the valley glimmered through at night, and stars were very close.

Our boys had won places in a scholarship school, University of Toronto Schools. Our maid, Jean, had her own room *and* bath, a luxury for our income group in those days, though we all had household help. My mother and father and adopted brother, Phil, had moved from Edmonton to my father's birthplace in Stratford, Ontario, a hundred or so miles distant. Our world seemed bright and warm and very snug. We had a big mortgage, but prospects for the firm were good.

History always has seemed to creep up on me suddenly, then wham! But then, it did on hundreds of thousands of Canadian homes as happy and full of promise as mine in that autumn of 1939.

Autumn came with a sweep of colour up the valley to waves of fear and apprehension in our hearts. That September, the week Canada entered war, Dick, like so many fellow university graduates everywhere in the country, reported for officer training. His whole architectural firm broke up for military service.

Our maid Jean was to leave. Hands were needed everywhere, in munition plants, on farms, in fruit- and vegetable-growing areas. I was one of the lucky wives, in my opinion (not my husband's), because an eye injury sustained playing cricket at school made him a turn-down for service overseas. I learned long after his death of some of the efforts he made to get over with so many of his friends. Not that he was a militant type. But we all had a cause we believed to be right and important and needed to share.

Strangely enough, the war years were to become among the most exciting of my life. With a wonderful husband-and-wife team finally installed in the top floor — housing was at a premium — (my study and their living-room, maid's bedroom, and bath adjoining) I was free, after a series of misadventurous part-time helpers, to move about.

This was to mean travelling both with Dick and on my own to many army, navy, and air force installations. Visiting munition plants, going to sea from Halifax in a minesweeper, travelling the country to do radio broadcasts to try to help conserve food. Visiting New York and Hollywood on Victory Drive stories.

I was to serve as a staffer with the Wartime Prices and Trade Board, write for *Chatelaine*, do regular broadcasts for the Canadian Broadcasting Corporation, and later became an editor in the newly established newsroom of the national network. It was a hectic, challenging period of my life.

Our lovely house became a liability with no public transportation near, a gasoline shortage, a small baby, and two young boys. Second lieutenant's pay didn't stretch very far, and even when Dick got his majority, it was a tough pull. We could see no end in sight to the hostilities. Before the war was far from over and I barely put down roots in my own and very special place, we had to sell 32 Bennington Heights Drive.

Nine

"God save the Queen," groaned one of the veteran BBC cameramen. He was heralding my arrival in the Toronto briefing room for Queen Elizabeth's most recent tour of Canada. My disaster-prone history on such safaris here, in Britain, and in the United States is legend. But first . . . .

There are always reunions of veteran media members from various countries when that very special brand of reporting I call royal camp-following brings them together. You form a bond, I guess, like soldiers sharing camouflage manoeuvres or prisoners planning tunnel breaks. (Not that British reporters don't try to feed the rest of us so-called off-the-record stuff about the Royals, hoping we'll write it so that they can throw up their hands in horror back home, quoting what we say. We're onto it, of course, and offer them equally fabricated tidbits about our own VIPs.)

The role of reporter in matters royal is as different from that of the customary news gatherer as is the operation of private eye from land surveyor. Your story is what you ferret out from behind the very parfait scene of every royal performance — over-transom or keyhole stuff, in a non-censorable way. And performance it is, a very set though movable period piece with endless stylized protocol, tradition, red tape, and crimson carpet rushed from one location to another and rolled out in the most unlikely places. If it is a play — and sometimes I expect at any moment all the crowned and medallioned characters, pompous aldermen plus wives, and puffed-up officials will fall down and turn into an Alice-in-Wonderland pack of cards — your sleuthing eye is focused as much on audience as stage.

Well-rehearsed and carefully timed theatrics featuring those Buckingham Palace superstars the Americans call Liz and Phil are there for everyone to see and hear, first-hand or on television. Your job, as reporter, is to catch what the public didn't have access to and to tell how they themselves behaved and reacted.

Majestic goings-on affect different royal-plumage watchers in different ways. Like many reporters who have trailed the Royals over long years, I always start out a sceptic. "This time, it won't work. I'll pierce the mystique." I never do. I've seen such seasoned and worldly press photographers as *The Toronto Star's* Reg Innell turn cow-eyed and putty-voiced when summoned to converse with Queen Elizabeth. I remember Dorothy Kilgallen, the New York-based syndicated columnist and once acerbic chronicler of peccadillos of the high, the mighty, and the wealthy of many lands, standing behind me in a line to be received by the Queen and Prince Philip. It was in Ottawa, and she had twitted some of us over our colonial obeisance to just another woman. "I'll give her some plain talk," she said, eyes snapping.

I turned back to watch the writer, after my own usual tongue-tied moments. She just stood there, mumbled something as she took the Queen's hand, looked into those cool, clear blue eyes, and curtsied. Her "yes, your majesty", and "no, ma'am", were as respectful as any I have heard. She walked away,bemused. "What is it?" she asked. "What does it do to you?"

My own theory revolves around the reach back into the mists of history of a long procession of royal personages, linked by blood — almost a race memory. It struck me vividly once when, with a small group of reporters and military personnel, I waited at a fairly primitive training camp in Manitoba, miles from anywhere.

The Queen and Prince Philip were to visit, and there we stood on the wide, blue-domed prairie. A ridiculous little strip of red carpet was laid out, leading to a flat square surrounded by fields of wild grasses and low stunted bush, and a sweet scent of wolf willow was on the wind. First a speck, then a winged shape, then a plane coming down until we could see the little royal standard blowing on the bow. The door opened, a colonel snapped to salute, and out stepped the smiling, perfectly groomed young woman whose ancestors had led troops in the Wars of the Roses and welcomed Wellington back from the Battle of Waterloo. Somehow it was to shiver, as though old and sceptred ghosts stirred in this new, raw country.

But here, too, is the untouchable, unreachable status. Like it or not, you can't buy or work or build your way to queenhood and kinghood. No amount of image-making, entrepreneuring, tub-thumping, or manipulation can give you access to the throne of the Monarch of the Commonwealth of Nations. Mind, a lot of lesser lights hope some of the royal magic will rub off, and I've seen men and women of so-called high estate so turned on by a slight brush with royalty that it's highly embarrassing to witness.

There's something else that should explain to many puzzled outlanders the sense of pride and property-right Britain still holds, by and large, for the institution of royalty. Not only is it a token of past glories and conquests, when Britain did, indeed, rule the waves and an empire on which the sun never set. The monarchy is a kind of security island in a world changing so rapidly, and often so alarmingly, that apprehension is one of the few constants. Yesterday's shady street of familiar old houses is today's monstrosity of sterile high-rises. Where we lately walked in a field of flower and birdsong, cars beetle along an eight-lane highway, spewing noxious gases. The friendly little grocery shop has vanished to imprison us in the chain-gang line-up of food-cart pushers in the supermarket, to be checked through by a cashier as mechanized as the register.

But Buckingham Palace, Clarence House, Balmoral, the Changing of the Guards, the Beefeaters in the Tower, and all the other familiar royal trappings are solid and unchanging.

Ah, and the colour and the sparkle of coronets and jewels, fairy princesses, robes and gowns, Graustarkian uniforms and epaulettes, in a world gone so grey and olive-drab. Perhaps, most of all, the pageantry. I have watched it from the days of the magnificent coronation of Queen Elizabeth II through to the wedding of her daughter Princess Anne to Captain Mark Phillips in Westminster Abbey not long ago. Millions saw that superbly orchestrated ceremony and parade on television and knew that here, at least, no one could touch the British for the sure grasp of panoplied discipline, training, and costuming.

One more reason for the reverence for royalty: the present Queen, who may not have the easy charm of her greatly loved mother, Elizabeth the Queen Mum, is such a pro at her job. She's very like her father King George VI, whose courage and example in World War II had as much effect on the morale of his people, I suggest, as did Winston Churchill's arrogant scorn of the "Nawzzies". "The King is still in London" — it was a rousing refrain of the days of the terrible Battle of Britain and the mass bombing of the British capital. His daughter is living up to her heritage.

What's she like, really? How about Prince Philip? Is Princess Margaret as . . . well, as unpredictable and wilful as they say? How about Lord Snowdon and the rest?

I'll begin with the present Queen Elizabeth, because we started together. Her Majesty was on her first visit to Canada, when she was still Princess Elizabeth and had but lately wed her handsome prince. I was on my first royal tour. That was in October of 1951. I was assigned by *The Globe and Mail*, where I then was a columnist, with two of the finest journalists I know and the most delightful friends and confrères — Kenneth MacTaggart and Bruce West. Around the office we became known as the trembling trio, on this as on many other assignments together, because of our constant apprehension when away from home base. I have found this a characteristic of most of the best journalists I know. It's like the skilled actor's stage fright or the great athlete's last-minute sense of panic.

This was to be a month-long tour, most of it by special train, with press cars coupled to the royal coaches. We were to stay with it all the way, from Quebec City to Victoria. We met the Princess all right at Dorval airport, Montreal, and she emerged from the stratocruiser, the *Canopus*, looking wan and frightened. (We realized later she was pregnant.)

In Ottawa, Mayor Charlotte Whitton, a firm royalist and fiery little feminist, had arranged for a royal flotilla to sweep along the Ottawa River, so that citizens and thousands of tourists flocking in could line the banks and get a good view of the young couple. Charlotte was in the gaily bedecked flagship with the Royals and their attendants and (I later learned) a radio on which they listened to the running story of their processional cruise. It was a cold November day, and a stranger sight than this strung-out, meandering, and motley aquatic parade would be hard to imagine.

The boat for the *national* press tour party (always a snobbish distinction from local scribes we picked up and dropped regionally) was one of the many power boats of ancient vintage commandeered for the occasion, its pilot a young and obviously inexperienced sailor. No sooner had we coughed and staggered into the procession than there were several clearly dying spasms of the rusty engine and we were adrift midstream. With a Herculean effort on some time-warped oars, men of the party painfully pulled us near shore at a point where a small wooden fisherman's clubhouse offered a rickety wharf.

Twin hazards menaced my next move. First, my eager-beaver instinct to reach the clubhouse and to telephone ahead of the others and file from notes I had made earlier. So near-sighted Dempsey outsmarted herself, because the second hazard was that, unbeknownst to this Torontonian, the Eddy Match Company up river spewed shavings from its product into the water. At the spot where we were attempting to land, they had eddied into a curve in the shoreline, forming a sawdusty mat. Thinking it was solid ground, I leapt from the boat while others waited for it to touch the wharf. Alas, it was *not* solid ground. Slowly I sank up to my shoulders in icy murk. An empty beer carton surfaced as I went down.

The roars of laughter from my fellow reporters, richly deserved, soon were stifled in concern, and I was hauled out, cold and singularly unlovely, webbed in matchwood and slime. A photographer of a rival paper snapped the sorry scene, but graciously did not send it in, due to my venomous threats. My friends hauled me to the clubhouse, where a fire was burning in a pot-bellied stove. There was no telephone, and so the others rushed off. A lone attendant tried to comfort me — none of the waiting taxis would take me in, quite wisely — and in a few moments a man who had been duck hunting drove up. Grudgingly he agreed to return me to the Lord Elgin Hotel. My heavy camel's-hair coat was crusted and sopping, and my plight was not eased by the fact that the hunter had covered his back seat with canvas (the only reason, I imagine, he agreed to a Samaritan gesture), strewn with the corpses of a dozen or so bloody wild fowl. By the time we arrived at the hotel, where he dropped me and fled, I looked like something out of a nightmare (or an Alice Cooper performance today). As I slunk through the lobby, the cluster of built-in paper-reading sitters who always populate such places glanced up, startled. Some hastily decamped. Several disappeared into the recesses of the beer parlour.

In the elevator, the operator stopped and stared as I stood, dripping water forming a pool at my feet. I said crossly, "Well, get me to the tenth floor. Have you never seen a wet woman before?"

Back in the gala procession, I was to find later, the Princess and Duke of Edinburgh heard this startling break in the flow of glowing description of golden-agers, some in wheelchairs, waving handkerchiefs; Scouts and Guides, Wolf Cubs and Brownies, marching ashore in pace with the onward convoy; crowds shouting and waving flags . . . "We interrupt this broadcast to report that one of the women reporters covering the royal flotilla from the press boat has just fallen into the river. That is all we have for now. So back to the Princess, who is looking radiant (I imagine she was stung with the stiff winter wind) . . . ."

And there the radio people left me. But word soon spread, and Bruce West and Kenneth MacTaggart, off on other aspects of the tour, rushed to a telephone. When they found me in my room, just emerging from a shower and wondering what I would wear to a reception later in the day (I had another dress, but just one coat), Bruce said, "But Lotie, you had a cold already."

"Well, it's gone now," I answered. And oddly, it was.

Next scene: a borrowed coat and word at the reception that the Princess would like to speak with me. She had ascertained the identity of the soggy reporter. Having learned from me that I was all right, Her Royal Highness allowed herself a mischievous smile. "Will you be coming with us on the whole tour, Miss Dempsey?" she asked, innocently.

"Yes, your Highness, I will."

She appraised me for a moment. "Might you not find it rather strenuous?" There were smiles all around, and so I gathered my courage and said, knowing she was new to our big and often astonishing country, "Not any more strenuous, ma'am, if I may be so bold as to suggest it, than you will."

I'm sure, if she later reflected on this observation, she would agree with it — after going down the mines, up the mountains, through the dust, and under the tent flaps of Canada. Not to mention unintentional confrontations with this reporter, such as the time I tripped, curtsying, and fell on Prince Philip. But that, later.

There was a postscript to my misadventure in the Ottawa River. My husband, who had been sitting at home reading while my small son listened to the tour report on the radio, was roused from his preoccupation with the child's remark, "Daddy, they say one of the women reporters just fell off the press boat into the river."

Without taking his eyes from his newspaper, my husband replied, "That will be your mother."

Ten

Poet Richard Le Gallienne wrote about "the great dying of great kings and queens". If royalty is a dying institution in Britain, which I doubt, the present royal family will be put under a microscope for history as were those of the last of the czars, the French Louis's, and Kaiser Wilhelm. They're an interesting bunch, when you get behind the figureheads and see them as state employees doing a job they either were born to or signed on for by way of the marriage bed.

Save your sympathy in the case of Queen Elizabeth and her heavy burdens of office. She likes the job, is good at it, and it's Her Majesty, not the often-maligned public officials in her wake, who sets the spit and polish character of events she graces. It is the Queen who not only approves days and evenings of programming that would exhaust a dray horse, but also frequently pencils in more. She likes things done punctiliously, punctually, and with dignity, and she is the first to bow to her own dictum.

The last time I saw them all together was at Princess Anne's wedding in Westminster Abbey, when the horsey and high-spirited young woman (suitably and demurely subdued) married commoner Captain Mark Phillips. My seat in the Abbey afforded an unimpeded view of an interesting family grouping in the chancel. As the impressive ceremony went forward, I found myself studying each member of this first of first families, and my mind started sorting little jigsaw pieces out of the composite.

Was the ghost of the Queen's and her sister Margaret's uncle, the Duke of Windsor, hovering in the candle-lit shadows of this holy house where he would, but for the woman he loved, have been crowned King of England? I had first shaken hands with the Prince of Wales, a slight, unimposing young man with those remarkable blue eyes characteristic of the family, as a young girl in Edmonton. We edged along a line-up at the legislative buildings and clasped the prince's left hand. (We thought it was a Boy Scout shake, but learned later his right had been immobilized by hearty Western grips.) Edmonton then had a rootin'-tootin' extroverted mayor named Joe Clark, a hearty man of the people whose grammar may have lacked a little polish. (Edmonton was just emerging from pioneer days, and one royal visitor to Government House was intrigued to find tiny pink, blue, yellow, green, etc., threads tied to knives and forks for a state dinner. This was accepted identification so that cutlery could be returned to the rightful owners, matrons of the town from whom it had been borrowed, when a guest list outstripped the on-hand supply of the Queen's representative, who had been an undertaker.)

Mayor Clark was determined to preside at a dinner for the Prince with as much protocol and as fitting a welcoming address as he would get anywhere in the British Empire. So he proceeded to recount a rather lengthy history of the royal line from which the guest of honour had descended, coming, finally, after much yawn-stifling among the diners, to these words: "And now, sir, to come to your Royal Highness's more immediate father."

I'm told that the Prince loved it. After that he refused to refer to King George in any other way than as "my more immediate father".

I was to have, I believe, one of the last audiences with the Duke of Windsor, by then an old man, on his final stay in New York in May of 1967. It was a wonderful hour, among the gilt and rococo of the hotel suite, filled with so many of their own treasures and massed with flowers. The Duchess was not present, and the Duke chatted amiably about any number of things. The face now, never strong or firmly characterized, was lined, and he looked very frail. But the eyes were as vividly blue as ever, and soon I was at ease.

Speaking of his Alberta ranch, he sighed, "I sold too soon, before they discovered oil and natural gas." He talked of Canada a great deal, and his love of my country. Yet he doubted he would be back, now . . . . "My nieces," he said, "love to go to Canada." I think he felt the end was near.

I came away feeling sad. There was such a gentle quality about him. Never tough enough, I thought, for kingship. Elizabeth has the stamina.

A great contrast to the Duke of Windsor is Prince Philip. Tall, still handsome, very masculine, the hint of Teutonic arrogance always there, never quite veiled. From early youth Philip was groomed by his uncle, Lord Louis Mountbatten, to be a queen's consort. Lord Louis has had a tremendous influence on the royal family, and, through Philip, on Queen Elizabeth.

I suspect he helped to orchestrate the courtship, knowing just when the time was for Philip to drive up breezily in his little car and call for Princess Liz. No question, she was very much in love with the dashing, polo-playing naval officer.

I remember once in Fort William (now Thunder Bay) at the Lakehead, a cold Sunday morning in November. They had not been married long, but were guardedly formal in public. They were booked in one floor of the hotel, and I had made an appointment to see the Princess's lady-in-waiting that morning to get some data on her British-designed wardrobe. (I always found I could get through by discussing British goods of one kind and another. All the Royals are star salespeople abroad.) We lingered longer than either of us had intended, and as I went to leave, the Princess and Prince Philip emerged from their suite down the hall. To shut the door would catch their attention, and my informant was not happy to have the royal pair know she had received me on this hallowed ground. So she put her finger to her lips, and we stood just inside, but able to watch them. As they moved along, Philip looked at Elizabeth's feet, then pointed with an accusatory cluck-cluck. She had no rubbers or overshoes, and so he left her there and went back. Unaware she was being observed, Elizabeth toed and heeled along the corridor like a happy child, swinging her purse and with eyes so full of love I felt guilty for watching. Philip came up, knelt, and put the rubbers on with the grace with which I later saw him pledge his fealty to his monarch at the coronation. Then they moved, arms entwined, to the elevator.

I came to have a great respect and admiration for this princess who became in every way a queen worthy of her father, the loved and dedicated George VI. And yet, when the crown tilted a little, so human.

Once I saw her laugh so unexpectedly and so infectiously that we all roared. It was at the opening of Expo in 1967 in Montreal. The Queen had had some very iffy times in Montreal and Quebec City, during a tour when the French-English problem was very tense, and there were complaints that people couldn't see enough of her because of a close guard, in addition to the usual flock of officials. Thus she suddenly decided to ride the overhead open cable car so that everyone could see her. By lucky accident, I was with an aide when the decision came and followed him to sit in the little car just behind the Royals. Away we went, swooping over the cheering throngs.

There had been no announcement, and so people in the buildings were not aware of the adventure. At one point, the car track swung right beside a roof-top restaurant in one of the Fair buildings. We happened to stop there for a minute. A man and woman were eating hot dogs and drinking pop at a window table, and the woman looked up to see the face of her Queen smiling on the other side of the glass. She choked and shook the man's arm. He waved a hand at her "joke" when you could see she was telling him of the sight ouside. Then he turned and looked, blanched, dropped his paper cup, jumped to attention and, so help me, curtsied. That was when the Queen roared — and waved with a regal nod.

Each time we would meet, the matter of my falling in the Ottawa River on her first Canadian visit would come up. Last time she said to me, mischievously, "I've wondered, Miss Dempsey, did you fall or were you pushed by fellow reporters?"

"No, ma'am. I was rushing to file my copy in the telegraph office."

She interrupted, "And you filed it in the river instead."

Prince Philip was not so amused the day I tripped on my own curtsy and fell against his shoulder. That can be explained, too. I was flustered when I was announced in a receiving line at Rideau Hall, the residence of the Canadian Governor-General and his wife in Ottawa. I always carry a purse with open sides, so that I can reach a notebook and pencil and any needed invitations without the fuss of opening the bag. I had tucked my presentation card in there, ready to be handed to the aide for announcement. But that day, just before coming to the reception, I'd gone to the beauty salon recommended by then Secretary of State Judy LaMarsh. I was pleased with the job and asked for the hairdresser's business card so that I could telephone next time I was in Ottawa. She gave me one — it was the Martha Gray Beauty

Salon or something such — and, fearing to be late, I dropped it in the open pocket.

So of course I handed the aide that card in the line-up, and he announced sonorously, "Martha Gray Beauty Salon." That's what threw me.

Philip is the one who makes the jokes. He likes to be one of the boys, going off in corners with the male reporters and passing along mildly off-colour stories — a kind of lavender locker-room camaraderie. (But let him tell the jokes, and don't be misled by the free and easy air. Once, on one of his airplane trips north, when there were just a handful of male reporters and it was a long, cold way from the palace and protocol, one of the reporters called him Philip. He was brought quickly into line.) Anyway, here's one of the jokes Philip told a reporter friend of mine, male gender. A British soldier posted at a very remote station in Scotland was brought before his commanding officer and accused of some barnyard behaviour with a sheep that was considered un-gentlemanly and un-British. His defence was, "Sorry, sir. I thought it was a WAAC in a mouton coat." That kind of thing.

His wit is often sharp and biting, sometimes at the expense of those of lesser station, like reporters, who cannot hit back. You may recall the time he turned the garden sprinklers on a group. He has a brilliant mind, an impressive presence, and could have been successful in any one of half a dozen fields.

The Queen Mum, Queen Elizabeth's mother, formerly Queen Elizabeth, is the undoubted love of people every-where she goes, and by all odds the public favourite in the royal family. She's warm, gay, and a kind of catalyst among the others. She loves donning the beautiful jewelled and embroidered gowns Sir Norman Hartnell designs for her (although that well-known couturier to royalty once sighed and told me, "I do wish the Queen Mum weren't so fond of chocolates. I have to do so much draping in spots.") When I last saw Hartnell, I asked if he felt badly at not doing Princess Anne's wedding gown, when he has designed nearly all the great-occasion wear of the Royals for so long. "Not really," he said with the wicked little smile he can produce. "She's quite young, you know, and not ready yet perhaps for . . . well, you know, a sense of presence. A young girl should look simple and she has time later for grandeur."

Hartnell also explained to me why the Royals wear off-the-face or small hats (except for Anne) — because people want to see their faces. When I commented that there was criticism of the Queen's lack of high style or fashion leadership, he said, "Don't you realize that every British woman whose husband is perhaps off in the service or doing some mundane job must feel that she could look as good as the Queen any day? This is part of relating. But at night, for the grand occasions, we can create gowns worthy of the jewels."

So the great Hartnell was sharing his long-time monopoly on regalia for the Royals on state occasions, here in Westminster Abbey, at Princess Anne's wedding.

As millions around the world who watched on television know, it was one of the most impressively spectacular events of modern times — indeed, perhaps the last richly jewelled, gowned, and panoplied hurrah of those born or wed to palace life in many countries. For struggling Britain of these later post-war years, it seemed almost a supreme final effort to display their historic pageantry, going out with a bang, not a whimper.

Yet, strangely, despite the power and the glory, Anne's wedding was very much a family affair. Where I sat in the Abbey, I had a clear close-up view of the family gathered in the chancelry. There was the Queen Mum, smiling and reassuring, touching Prince Charles's hand and keeping an eye on the young ones in the back row who were carefully supervised by the Duchess of Kent. It was a full family portrait in the splendour of a state occasion, perhaps one of the last we shall see. The only ones who seemed out of key and in discordant note were Princess Margaret and her husband Lord Snowdon. It was more than a natural anxiety that their young daughter, nine-year-old Lady Sarah Armstrong-Jones, would correctly execute her demanding role as attendant. (She did.) As everyone else in the royal party smiled and followed the service intently, Margaret and Tony seemed very sombre, almost detached. It was hard to believe that this dour-looking, plump woman was the same sparkling, blue-eyed young matron I had followed, only ten years before, on her dream-visit to America. But that's a story in itself, for it took us to Hollywood, as well as San Francisco, Washington, and New York, and to the most "pinch me" day of my long life in the news media.

Eleven

The greatest instant extravaganza I ever saw in Hollywood never was recorded on film. It was a party at Universal Studios on a Friday in November 1965. Princess Margaret and Lord Snowdon were in the midst of a tour of the U.S.A. that I was covering for *The Toronto Star*. But why this should be such a memorable happening in the far-from-humdrum life of the Queen's younger sister is worth a little probing before we join the festivities.

But for her high birth, Margaret might have been a performer herself. That would never do. (It's lucky for Princess Anne her passion is riding. Pure-bred horses have almost as much status as blue-blood humans in present royal circles. The Queen and her mother are breeders and knowledgeable race fans; Philip and Charles are avid polo players.) So Princess Margaret, a wonderful mimic — especially right-on with Churchill and Baldwin — and a more than passable pop pianist, has had to content herself in the use of the royal prerogative to enjoy the company of the many stars of stage, screen, and television she likes, admires . . . and perhaps envies.

As she told us often on this first tour of the United States, it had been the dream of her life to visit such storied new-world cities as New York, San Francisco, and, oh most especially, Hollywood.

Of course, all play makes for questions in the British House of Commons when taxpayers are footing the bill, and so Meg and Tony's itinerary also included paying respects to President and Mrs. Lyndon Johnson in the White House and visits to British trade exhibits, museums, art galleries, hospitals, and homes for the aged and indigent.

I had many revealing insights into the pair, their diverse tastes and interests, and came home liking Lord Snowdon best of all·the men in the royal circle since King George VI. He is most certainly the best informed in all the arts, the most sensitive and responsive to beauty and excellence, both natural and man-made. And his is a shy, almost gentle courtesy and thoughtfulness in dealing with those of stations lowlier than his marriage achieved.

It could be just another of the Birtish media's stories, but there is a persistent contention that, when Tony was squiring Margaret around, it was suggested to him by someone in authority at Buckingham Palace that if his intentions were serious, they would be well received. For a free-wheeling young man, a very talented photographer, and part of an unregimented, creative element in the British scene, this would mean a very different life. But then, it did put one in . . . well, Tony proposed. After their marriage he broke tradition, stubbornly, by accepting a job as photographer on Lord Thomson's *Sunday Times* and hasn't been given the sack to date.

I once asked Lord Thomson's son, Ken, if it had been a status thing to get a princess's husband on the *Times*. "Don't you believe it," Ken said firmly. "Dad likes the Royals, but he's too good a businessman and too hard-headed for that.

And Snowdon has a far bigger finger in the *Sunday Times* than appears on the surface. As for time off for royal duties, he's always working 'between the ears'."

There had been some belittling remarks about "the bird cage Tony built for the London Zoo" as a rather trifling project for a royal family member to be involved in. So one day in Washington, when Margaret was to be given a reception somewhere and Tony was going to visit the zoo, I opted for Tony.

Only four or five of us joined him on this venture, and as the director took him around, I was able to move beside them. Snowdon's knowledge of aviary structures and his talk of flight patterns and habits of different species was highly impressive. (His "bird cage" was as advanced an aviary as any designed today; people may walk among the exciting flutter and sweep of wings. I suspect his second choice to photography would have been architecture.) We were a pleasantly informal little group, as Tony has none of Philip's don't-come-too-near attitude.

Margaret frequently was late, as she has been on occasions I have covered in Canada, and certainly has not the consideration for others to be found in both the Queen and the Queen Mother. I remember one evening at a performance of the Stratford (Ontario) Shakespearean Festival. There were times when the diamond pendants on her ears dropped suspiciously, and there was a suggestion of a gentle sound of dozing. No one is commanded to like Shakespeare, and there is little question that her tastes run more to musical comedy and other lighter forms of entertainment. But there was no excuse for her remarks at a post-performance meeting with the cast backstage. The most charitable assessment would be that they were thoughtless. Perspiring actors still in costume and grease paint lined up to be presented to the Queen's sister. They had given their all — and from the day Sir Tyrone Guthrie first set the pattern for performances there, it has been a top-standard all. Margaret stood as they waited to bow and curtsy, and there was a silence ready for her words.

"I was fascinated," she said, "by the thrust stage and the design of the theatre."

Have you ever seen an artist's face when someone told him his picture had a perfectly lovely frame?

This was in pre-Tony days and not too long after the widely publicized break-up of her romance with her father's equerry, the tall, charming war hero with whom she had fallen in love. As a father with a broken marriage, Peter Townsend was considered unsuitable, and Margaret bowed to public pressure and, one suspects, to the strong disapproval of both the Queen and Prince Philip. Watching Margaret since and seeing the changes in her, especially in the past few years, I feel she should have been allowed to marry Townsend. Today she might very well be permitted to do so, now that other divorces have touched the royal establishment. Townsend obviously was highly acceptable to the family, until Margaret fell in love with him. He was devoted to the King, and Margaret loved her father very dearly. There was, even then, little chance she would succeed to the throne. Yet the Duke of Windsor and his Duchess were often in the news and the Duke's defection from kingship to marry the American woman divorcee had been a considerable blemish around the Commonwealth.

Margaret was pictured as the gay young jet-setter princess. Perhaps her natural sense of fun and enjoyment, as a girl and young woman, was unduly underlined by her older sister's solid propriety.

At the time of her American tour, Margaret was maturing into a rich beauty, where before she had been merely pretty. She's the tiniest of the royal women, and then her waistline could, as they say, be encircled by a wedding ring. She had outgrown the bizarre hairdos, clothes, and hats she once wore and was beautifully and simply dressed in the daytime, a truly sparkling princess at night. Her eyes are the most beautiful of any of the typically blue-eyed family. They are closer to the violet-blue of Elizabeth Taylor's than the clear blue of her sister and mother.

So what happened to this beautiful, animated woman? How did she become the plump, dour matron I saw in the Abbey at Anne's wedding?

I got my first clues at the Museum of Modern Art in New York, when she paid a morning visit. Asked for her preference in beverage, she replied, "Gin and orange." Coffee, tea, etc., had been prepared, but at that hour, there wasn't any gin in the environs. So there was a tremendous flurry behind the scenes until somehow someone found the ingredients.

Between New York and Hollywood, there had been the most tremendous balls and parties. For you must remember, despite some of the disgruntled words I heard, Americans love royalty — almost any royalty or connection with same, however distant. I've rarely interviewed even the reigning superstars of stage, screen, concert hall, and television across the border without their mention of a command performance for British royalty as the ultimate stamp of professional status.

So now, in Hollywood that day at Universal Studios, the whole galaxy of famous film stars was to gather to salute the Princess Margaret.

At the time, I described the setting:

> Universal spent half a million dollars within the 200 by 175 foot cavernous studio, which had a ceiling aglow with masses of lights and equipment, emblazoning a fabulous piazza and gardens. Kensington Palace, the royal residence in which the Princess dwells in London, never was like this.
>
> As the Royal party entered the pillared doors of the stage, guests were seated at hundreds of tables for eight, each centred with a tall standard

filled with spicy white carnations on pale yellow linen . . . . From the patio the Princess descended wide steps into the great sunken garden carpeted in grass (studio-created, naturally) and completely surrounded by thousands of flowering mums, carnations, and blooming mimosa, planted in gardens backed by tall cypress trees.

The Royal table, also for eight, was on a raised dais far down the garden, overlooking a pool of deep blue water (dyed, it was admitted) with water lilies afloat.

The pool was flanked at either end by sparkling fountains in their own flower gardens — and in the centre of all this, seemingly floating on water, was a round platform on which Disneyland's famed brass band, complete with Sousa-style uniforms, played.

It was on that day I think I saw the beginning of what would be the sadness of Margaret today. All eyes were on Hitchcock as he directed Julie Andrews in a scene from *The Torn Curtain*. At least, I didn't notice anyone except me slip around to where Tony was talking with a cameraman about some film work, just behind where Princess Margaret was seated. Tony had left her, and for moments she was alone. She reached back and spoke to him. He looked up, smiled, and went on with his absorbed conversation. Then she reached back and touched him, beckoning with an imperious finger. He came around, his face set, leaned over, and whispered to her. Then he went back to the cameraman, and I could see the anger in her face.

That party was one of the last bursts of technicolour fireworks in a dying Hollywood. But glittertown was wonderful while it lasted, as we'll see, next chapter.

Twelve

There was the brilliant but outrageous British actor, Charles Laughton, edging his way excitedly on his knees around the Hollywood living-room of Canadian writer Norman Reilly Raine.

It was at Sunday brunch, with a small party of movie executives as guests, and Raine had recently delivered to the flamboyant Laughton his script for *Mutiny on the Bounty*, in which the actor was to play the infamous Captain Bligh. Laughton had the script in hand, reading and acting the role in his inimitable, drawling tones with the whiplash endings, moving to one after another of the company to have them hear his interpretation.

At the Raines' I was equally impressed at tasting hot broiled grapefruit and baked bananas — both new to my prairie-bred palate. The Raines were very good to me, and I met many of the stars through Norman, who cheerfully trundled me along to studios, film-lot commissaries, and my first visit to Sardi's, a favourite eatery in that glamorous era of the movies.

I had been presented for his thoughtful and kindly guidance by his old friend Napier Moore, then editor of *Maclean's* and editorial director of *Chatelaine*. I was *Chatelaine*'s feature editor. At the time, we were in the throes of World War II, and Hollywood was churning out fantasy and adventure — escape from the horrors of real life in the fighting theatres overseas.

Raine's fiction series about a hard-boiled but soft-hearted old girl on the waterfront called Tugboat Annie had been a tremendous hit in the *Saturday Evening Post*. So he was summoned to Hollywood as consultant on the film starring Canadian-born actress, Marie Dressler, who three years earlier had starred in a film with a young actress newly arrived from Sweden, Greta Garbo. Raine remained in Hollywood to live and work on other films, including *A Bell for Adano*.

Everyone who came in contact with the beautiful and mysterious Garbo found compellingly magnetic the fusion of ice and flame that was her personality. She cast a kind of spiritual hypnosis.

I remember a story, told me by a New York writer, about Garbo and the effect she had on men. He had spent a weekend at a country house in Connecticut, and the actress was among fellow guests. He eagerly accepted her proposal of an early Sunday morning walk in the countryside. They started out, Garbo in sweater, sturdy skirt, stout shoes, kerchief around her head, no make-up.

"She was so hauntingly beautiful I could hardly keep a steady pace," he said. "And she set a swift one. Once, as we were passing a field with a number of sheep and lambs she stopped, pointing to a lone little black ewe among the snowy ones.

" 'You know,' she said in those deep, gutteral tones, 'I think if that little black lamb could run out and across the road to us, the war would be over.' "

He smiled at my gasp of amazement and went on, "And

honest to heaven, for that moment I believed her. She did that to you."

In California I visited many sets to watch filming, but Garbo would allow no outsiders on hers. I saw her only once at close range. It was in the china-and-linen section of Burdine's department store in Los Angeles, and the star had long since stopped making films. I was discussing some place mats with a saleswoman when I realized she had stopped speaking. Furthermore, a complete hush had fallen over the area. When I looked up, there was the great one, swinging along with her easy stride, stopping to touch a piece of china. I was reminded of Conrad Aiken's lines "Your hands once touched this table and this silver . . . They knew you once, O beautiful and wise." Californians are the most avid autograph collectors I have ever seen. Yet here everyone stood where they were. No one approached. She moved on and away. Yes, she was as fascinating as any human I have ever seen.

The old Hollywood was a kind of tinsel cocoon, from which emerged so many gorgeous butterflies, glittering creatures that flew high and fast . . . then too often fluttered earthwards, wings broken. I interviewed many on their short and giddy sweeps and have forgotten most of their names. I remember once, though, going to a set for a story on a voluptuous little blonde, Gloria De Haven. She had just finished a picture with a skinny young Italian-American crooner, lately of the Tommy Dorsey band. While waiting for Miss De Haven I made polite conversation with him, mentioning that I had heard him with the band. He spoke, with curled lip, about a snake. There was no further enlightenment. It may or may not have had to do with problems the bobby-sox idol had had in easing out of a contract with the Dorsey band. I asked him if he would mind standing out of the way while I had my photographer take a picture of Miss De Haven. (His name was Frank Sinatra. So much for my crystal ball.)

Lotta with Gloria De Haven and make-up artist. ("Fading boy-singer" Frank Sinatra not pictured.)

Lotta with Bing Crosby early in World War II.

Lotta with Cary Grant on the set of "Shining Future",
which was made during World War II.

Lotta all dressed up for a bit part on the Bonanza set in
the early 1960s with Michael Landon and Lorne Greene.

For the accredited reporter or columnist (read: one with a big enough readership) Hollywood was a land of wine and honey, the wine sometimes spiked and the honey well combed with press agentry. But it was tremendous fun to me, at least.

There was an air of informality, almost haphazardness, about the studios in those early days, and you could sit around and watch interminable takes under the harsh, enervating lights. I liked talking with the cameramen, script girls, make-up experts, clothes and set designers, so often the genies of the magic lamp of filmdom. But even the most skilled could work no more than a passing miracle without some kind of super quality in the object of their adornment, as many a fallen "star" can attest. It's the thing Sinatra proved he had, when the fading boy-singer emerged as a great actor in *From Here to Eternity*.

Once I was watching a star then considered the most beautiful in cinema land. (She has since, sadly, faded to impoverished ignominity.) At a break, I asked the chief cameraman who had been shooting close-ups of this seemingly perfectly moulded creature if she had any "bad" angles he had to watch, as so many had. He shook his head.

"You can shoot her from here . . . from there . . . from anywhere. Right up to her perfect nose." There was a kind of awe in his tone one seldom heard from technical people. Then he added, nonchalantly, "Actually, she's a bitch. Ah, but what a bitch!"

The only male star I saw in those days who could freeze even a company of his stellar peers into immobility was the actor rightly known as the King — Clark Gable. When he came into the commissary at Metro-Goldwyn-Mayer, everyone simply fell silent, and those who knew Gable gave an almost reverential salute. This man exuded sex and virility as I have seldom seen it. It was almost an animal thing, and even the most Victorian lady would have had to hang onto her cool not to follow, if beckoned, to the nearest sheltered privacy.

I was covering the Academy Awards in the days at the old Grauman's Chinese Theater, when they were so informal you could jump on stage afterwards and interview the Oscar winners. I remember thus talking with Jennifer Jones, Charles Coburn, Paul Lukas, Herbert Marshall, and a dozen others — but most especially Greer Garson, who has the most astonishing green eyes I've ever seen, particularly with that auburn hair. I was also greatly impressed with a young singer who came out to do a song called "Honeysuckle Rose". She was in a slim café-au-lait satin gown and her name was Lena Horne. I looked at my program again. "Lena Horne — remember that," I said to myself. For she was amber honey all over, voice, face, and all, and every time I see that great artist in the full bloom of magnificently fulfilled maturity I remember. Last time I caught her show, with Tony Bennett in Toronto, she was simply magnificent. Yet she had looked just as good, earlier in the day, when I ran into her hurrying into the exhibition from China in the Royal Ontario Museum, a woolly toque pulled almost over the flashing eyes.

There was another newcomer to the Hollywood scene during one of my early visits there, a young man just seduced from his first big successes on Broadway, with an unbelievable variety of talent. He could dance, sing, act, play romantic leads, and send off such sparks they ignited everything in sight. I wrote a glowing report back to *Chatelaine* about this fabulous performer whose name, I am embarrassed to note, I hadn't quite caught. To my eternal shame, I referred to the one and only Danny Kaye as Sammy Kaye (a band leader). And despite the magazine's flock of proofreaders and researchers, my story went through with Danny as Sammy all the way. You can see he was just emerging.

As a reporter, I try never to let my personal feelings about a subject cloud his image, if it is a sound one. Entertainer beyond peer Danny Kaye certainly is. But in later years of personal interviews I have found him consistently rude and given to using his sharp and often biting wit at the expense of others, just for laughs.

Kaye was in Toronto in 1966 to publicize something or other — it could have been on behalf of his tremendous work with UNICEF for children around the world — and after a few sharp retorts to some questions of mine, to the entertainment of those who cared to laugh, I decided to set him up. He had been talking of his interest in Canada and affection for our great country, and so I asked him if he knew what important event was going to happen in the year 1967. (Our centennial, celebrated especially by Expo '67 in Montreal.)

Kaye thought for a moment, then said fliply, "Of course. Danny Kaye coming to Toronto to appear with your fine symphony orchestra."

For once I saw him uncomfortable in the laughs that followed. It just happened that kings, queens, heads of state, and famous people from every country in the world were coming to Canada in 1967.

As I said, it was a happy, often zany time in Hollywood in those years of superstars and super-studios. I was lucky to be invited home by a number of those I met, and often there were surprises. It was wartime, and at the Hollywood canteen, the most beautiful and talented of the world's spoiled darlings served coffee and sandwiches and (who knows) sometimes tea and sympathy to servicemen. There was a wave of saving and producing badly needed foodstuffs. Still, it was a little surprising to have Ann Sheridan, a lovely star of the day, take me home to see her new pig trough. Whether it was ever actually put to use I never knew. Another popular film star, Ruth Hussey, who had married an American army officer, had furnished a simple city house with more frills and ruffles than I had ever seen before. Still, nice perhaps for a fighting man to come home to.

Not long ago I was laughing with Gail Patrick, another glamour-puss of her day, over *her* hobby. When I first met her she had already left the screen and was operating a children's specialty shop in Hollywood. (A brilliant executive, Miss Patrick later was to become producer for the long-run *Perry Mason* detective series on television.) She invited me home, and I was intrigued with her small but perfect house. Then she took me to the kitchen to see her special wartime conservation project. There was a gadget on the window, which overlooked a hill with a barn-like structure at the top, some distance away.

"Look!" she said, with the delight of a child. She pulled the gadget, and a flap lifted in one part of the back building. Then, along a gently sloping narrow trough there rolled a white hen's egg, arriving, unbroken, to slide gently into a container on the sill. "My hens lay enough for me and my friends," she said proudly. At what cost, in the heart of expensive, elegant Beverly Hills, one can only imagine.

In the razzle-dazzle of the Hollywood that was, there are clear mountain peaks of experience vivid to this day. One was my meeting with the fine and honest Ingrid Bergman, whose star grows brighter with every passing year.

The Swedish actress had not been long in Hollywood — though long enough to have her picture on the cover of *Time* — when I was visiting. My request for an interview was received in a manner new to me then, and in a way I have never encountered since. "Miss Bergman would like some samples of your work," the studio press agent said. I obliged. In a day of two he called my hotel, surprise in his voice. Apparently this was a new approach to him, too.

"Miss Bergman would be happy to meet you for lunch." I asked when and where and he added, with real amazement, "She says to come to her home. It wouldn't be very satisfactory just meeting in the studio or a restaurant." I like to think she felt, from stories I had written, that I tried to get behind the make-up to the real person.

Bergman greeted me at the door wearing a simple sweater and skirt. Her little daughter, Pia, was there, coming in from play in a pair of worn coveralls. It was a simple suburban apartment with modern Swedish furniture. Once I crossed the threshold, I might have been visiting a friend in my own neighbourhood. Miss Bergman served lunch, a salad and rolls, from her neat kitchen. She has a scrutinizing gaze and such basic honesty that it forms almost a visible aura about her. She had been Sweden's greatest star, and at this time her accent was still fairly pronounced. We talked about her Hollywood experiences. She laughed.

"You know," she said, once we had established a kind of rapport, "the second day on the set the producer came over and said, 'Hello, darling.' I was so surprised and upset. I thought, 'What does this mean?' In Sweden it will be a very long time before you shall call anyone darling, and then you shall mean it. I think you are like that in Canada, yes?"

I said, quite legitimately then, in 1944, "Yes."

She nodded. "I have soon find that it means nothing at all. For by night-time the script girl and the director and the telephone operator and the drugstore clerk who sells me a soda — they have all called me darling or dear or honey. And I have discovered already that this does not have any special significance. It is just Hollywood."

I have met Bergman at press conferences since, and I think she still does not use words of endearment freely. In my story I wrote that she must be the most honest human being I had met in the film world. I still thought so when she went to Italy and had a child by the Italian film director, Roberto Rossellini, whom she was later to marry. Such behaviour wouldn't raise an eyebrow now, but then it was an international scandal.

I didn't see her in those years, but I did pick up a sad comment on the unhappy union as it later developed. At a Toronto supper party one night, during the period of that marriage, I found myself seated beside the famed violinist,

Jascha Heifetz. He and his wife had lived next door to Bergman and her then husband, Dr. Peter Lindstrom, in California.

When Heifetz was in Rome for a concert, Ingrid and her new husband invited her former neighbours to dinner in a restaurant.

"He tried to bring her down all the time," Heifetz said, scornfully. "He wasn't big enough for her. I thought at times she was near tears."

It was with great joy that I observed the actress in New York with her present husband, theatrical producer Lars Schmidt. This, I thought, was the ideal mating. He seemed a big man, thoughtful, a true liege man for a great woman.

This is as good a time as any for a confession. For years I felt the maddest kind of affection for perhaps the most loved man in Hollywood over long decades, Jack Benny. My infatuation went back to the radio days of the Benny tribe, when Sundays were the greatest nights of the week and millions of families gathered to hear the Jello Show with Jack Benny, then the incomparable Fred Allen and Allen's Alley, Phil Harris and Alice Faye, and finally that marvellously erudite man, Clifton Fadiman, and his friends, who discussed the arts. All in one night's listening, and more stimulating than most of television I have seen since.

Benny had been in Toronto playing the big O'Keefe Centre on his birthday, February 14, and so I wrote a column "To my Favourite Valentine". He liked it and called, suggesting that if I came to Hollywood I visit him at his Beverly Hills home. The day I spent there was as hilarious as it was moving.

I arrived in the morning, and Benny, still in pyjamas and dressing-gown, was just finishing his regular two-hour practice on his Stradivarius. We had several hours of intensely interesting conversation, and he explained earnestly that he really wasn't at all like the radio and television character he had so indelibly imprinted on the public mind. He was calm, collected, well organized — and of course, not really concerned about saving every penny.

In the course of the day, Vladimir Horowitz called long-distance from London to confirm an appearance Benny was to make with the London Philharmonic. There was some static on the line and Benny started feverishly clicking the receiver, calling for a maid (Mary, his wife, was in their Palm Beach place), running from one telephone to another, and finally climbing up on a bookcase and shouting excitedly at the maestro. He spoke of selling the lovely Beverly Hills place, and when I said that would be a shame, he asked me anxiously if I realized how much it cost to keep up? He took me to see his swimming pool, then led me by the hand on tiptoe to a fence.

"You won't believe who my next-door neighbour is!" he said eagerly, waiting for the look of surprise on my face. "It's Lucille Ball. And we just might get a glimpse of her."

I had interviewed Miss Ball at some length in a New York hotel suite, and I preferred Benny. It would never occur to him that this might be so.

When I spoke of his golf, an outdoor pleasure shared by his great friends, Bob Hope and Bing Crosby, he said, rather wistfully, "You know, I envy Bing and Bob. They really love golf. I just play a bit for exercise and something to do."

Music was his great love, and when we went to his study, lined with autographed photographs of the honoured and the mighty, men and women of high estate in every field of endeavour, it was the pictures of Benny taken with the great musicians of our time to which he pointed with the greatest satisfaction. But I left feeling a sadness for the man who had brought so much laughter to so many, and never with malice or meanness of any kind.

Not long ago I was talking with Milton Berle about his own autobiography. Although he lit into a number of people therein, his affection for Benny was obvious. At the time,

Benny had just died, and when I mentioned his name tears filled Berle's eyes.

"There was only one Jack," he said, "and one of the last times I saw him, he called me." (Berle acted out everything, as so many performers do.)

"Miltie?" Jack said.

Berle said, "Yes. Who's calling? (I knew, of course. Who could mistake that gentle drawl?)"

"It's Jack."

Milton paused. "Jack who?"

Benny identified himself. "I wondered if you were going to the so-and-so's Christmas Eve party?"

Milt said he and his wife were.

"Oh," said Benny, then stopped.

"I know, Jack," Milton said. "Mary isn't going and you thought . . . . Sure, we'll pick you up." (Mary seldom went, and this too was a loneliness.)

Milton continued, "We arrived at this producer's house and a maid came to take our coats. Jack looked into the crowds of glamorously dressed people, drinking and talking. He turned to me, looking ruefully after his disappearing outer garment. 'Any time, Milt,' he said, already thinking of home."

And Berle added, soberly, "He was a fine artist and a meticulous, hard-working professional. That off-the-cuff informal way he performed could never fool a fellow pro."

Just as interesting as the stars were the people behind the scenes who made so much of the magic of the shadow box. Edith Head, the great designer of fabulous clothes for the stars, spoke of how she "corrected" certain little figure flaws of many of the great. In that connection, when I was serving with the Wartime Prices and Trade Board of Canada, we once had the brilliant idea of getting some mementoes of the Hollywood greats for some sort of show or auction we were putting on. (Just how this fitted into finding housing, getting people to be honest about ration cards, saving sugar and butter, keeping price ceilings clamped on precious goods, I don't know. But there we were.) One of the items supplied was a sarong from the pin-up star, Dorothy Lamour. She was in all those *Road to . . .* pictures with Bob Hope and Bing Crosby, and the sarong, cleverly draped to accentuate the sexy figure, was her trademark.

Apparently it had been sent by a careless costumer from the studio. I can recall vividly the wails of anguish from men on our staff when it arrived and was shaken out to reveal a very substantial built-in padded bra.

I especially enjoyed a session, and visit at home, with Cedric Gibbons, a brilliant Prix de Rome architect who was Metro-Goldwyn-Mayer's star set designer. He was a big, down-to-earth type, who did sets for stylish pictures like *When Ladies Meet* and *The Women*, some of which set the pattern for homes all over the United States and Canada.

We were a movie-going country then and took much of our lead in styles of various kinds from the flicks. I remember a whole grade-six class of little well-fed, scrubbed-faced prairie girls appearing one Monday, to the bemusement of our teacher, with hair in tight little curls all over our heads. It was the pineapple bob Constance Bennett had displayed at the Bijou Saturday matinee.

Joan Crawford's padded shoulders weren't that difficult. Wads of cotton batten did the job, if sometimes precariously. For some of us, this wide-mouthed teen-ager included, the Mae Murray bee-stung lips were more difficult. And the flat-chested flapper era, when some of us were just blossoming into well-developed young women, was almost catastrophic. We bound bath towels firmly around our chests and pinned them with big safety pins for night-time slumbers. And I, for one, tried to bunch up my lips by applying adhesive tape at bedtime. Fortunately mothers, tip-toeing in to check on lights out found some of us torturing ourselves with these devices and put a firm stop to the nonsense.

Humphrey Bogart and Lauren Bacall with "the potted palm" (also known as Lotta Dempsey) during World War II.

But Cedric Gibbons laughed at the discomfiture he caused, especially to many a husband, by the wave of "modernistic" clearing out of living-rooms by many house-wives after seeing his glamorous sets.

"What they didn't realize," he told me, "was that we have to clear rooms to make way for the cameras. And besides, the room never could dominate the actors." He told me he had thousands of letters asking for plans for various houses in films he designed. "People don't realize we don't have plans for a complete house or even a room. Often it can stop just at the point the camera is going — like a door or even half a chair. And we can use bizarre or spectacular effects and colours. After all, these make-believe rooms and houses don't have to be lived in year after year. Anyway, I can't understand women wanting to sweep out their houses and re-do them all the time. I'm a comfort man myself."

Indeed he was, with a perfectly charming house, very traditional.

Hardest interview I ever did? Bogey. Yup, the great Humphrey Bogart. The day I was to see him he had just begun to get acquainted with a new leading lady, a tall, mocking model who had come from New York.

He was so besotted with the charm of that angular, witty young woman — a real challenge after all the soupy, goo-goo-eyed dames who had been pursuing him — he simply couldn't speak with any intelligibility to anyone else. A fly-by-night affair? Well, you judge. Her name was Lauren Bacall. And the photo I have of the three of us (she wasn't even supposed to be in the picture) is revealing — Bogey, Lauren, and something that might have been a potted palm that had somehow got into the act. That's me, the one out in the cold.

Thirteen

You never know when you're riding a wave of history — until the tide comes in.

As I've watched the surge and strength of the women's liberation movement, I've looked back and marvelled how I could have been so close to its beginning here in Canada (apart from the franchise) without real comprehension. I suppose it was because the famous Alberta Five — stubborn pioneers who fought and won a battle to get women into the Senate — simply were friends I ran into all the time.

They were Judge Emily Murphy, first woman judge in the British Empire; the Honourable Irene Parlby, first woman cabinet minister; Nellie McClung, ex-MLA, writer, and lecturer; Mrs. Henrietta Edwards and Mrs. Louise McKinney, community workers and club leaders. A small but powerful band who shaped and honed their case all the way from a modest Edmonton living-room to the Privy Council in London, England, where they triumphed in 1929. (Many years later, I was in on an anti-war movement called Voice of

Women. I knew what we were up to then. It was formed around my dining-room table.)

When the Alberta Five were busy with their dreams and schemes, I was very young. And it is often the young, rather than the mature, who say it can't happen here. Or who haven't patience or guts to plough the long furrow with faith in a far-distant vintage. So it was because she was a merry, roly-poly little woman who had a warm, hospitable home and often "included me in" when she had distinguished guests (like suffragette Emmeline Pankhurst) that I came to spend so much time with Emily Murphy. I was in my early twenties and she was older than my mother, but I had many friends among women of her ilk.

During my early years as a reporter in Edmonton, I came to know Emily very well and, as we both had a deep love of poetry, often dropped over to read and listen and to enjoy the always well-provisioned table of "the Reverends". Anglican clergyman Arthur Murphy was a gentle man, a perfect foil for the bubbling, energetic Emily, with his own quiet sense of humour. He had been a fiery enough preacher in his younger days, taking his little bride from Cookstown, Ontario, on a strenuous series of evangelical gospel sessions both on this continent and abroad. Then he had a parish in Manitoba, later settling permanently in the pioneer prairie town of Edmonton.

Emily, who used the pseudonym Janey Canuck in writing for magazines and newspapers, became known throughout Canada for her vivid, often irreverent, punchy prose. She was a reformer — her weapons, vitality and humour. Her pieces stand up well today, and she was a skilled platform lecturer.

Often I would go to court to watch her on the bench. There were times when she practically dragged me in to hear the sad and terrible things that could happen to people, many victims of circumstance or ignorance. I learned here of bestiality, child and wife beating, fathers raping their own terrified young daughters. The vicious, the betrayers, the men sometimes more animal than human were afraid of her tough sentences and lashing tongue. But her sympathy for the innocent and the misbegotten was equally recognized.

"You are young," she said to me once, seeing how shaken I was by the inhumanity of what I had seen and heard that day. "But know and care about these things if you are going to be a good reporter and, more important, a worthwhile human being."

There was a kind of crazy Irish ritual to our sessions in the warmth of her home, with its fine old family furnishings and walls of books. We would have tea (ah, that gooseberry and ginger jam, those toasted English muffins). Then she would often wind up the phonograph and play one of her favourite records — something like the then popular *Abdul the Bulbul Emir*, a terribly long narrative of the rivalry between Abdul and Ivan Skavinsky Skavar. She would sing along (off key) or dance around alone, her tiny feet light as any child's under the long skirt.

Then up to her study where, with chuckles and snorts and a tiny round fist pounding the table, she would bring me up to date on the latest gambit in her fight to get the British North America Act interpreted so that women could be accepted as "persons" and thus eligible for the Senate.

"You must follow me," she would say if my attention wandered (she had a fine legal mind and grasp of, to me, unintelligible technicalities), "because when you are as old as I am, you will see the harvest. This is a side door, but when women get this kind of authority and confidence, we'll get more of them out on the hustings fighting the political battles they must fight to take their rightful place in the government of this country."

It was a beautiful, fantastic plot, in which she was much aided by her brothers, the Ontario Ferguson men, who were lawyers and enjoyed the discomfiture of the long-time all-male citadel of male chauvinism, the Senate Chamber in Ottawa.

As I say, I knew all the women involved in the struggle, but both Irene Parlby and Nellie McClung told me later that Emily was the driving force, they merely willing adherents. What I remember, especially, was the fun and excitement they had. All were family women, good neighbours, and not a sobersides or a man-hater, *per se*, in the lot.

Emily, the brilliant strategist, deliberately chose just this type of woman, with an eye to each one's public following in a variety of fields and endeavours. As the brief for recognition was bombed down in each higher court of Canada, these women, always aided and abetted by the Ferguson brothers, simply carried on to the next one up until finally, triumph and a parade through the streets of London when the Privy Council decreed that women, indeed, were persons.

The last time I saw Emily Murphy, she was growing older and unwell. Heavily, the little feet no longer lilting, she took me up to the study. There she read me a letter she had just finished, to be read to her family at their regular Sunday dinner at the Murphy house after she was gone. (She had two daughters, one married with a child.) It was a warm and wonderfully moving communication — witty as always. I wanted to tell her she mustn't do it — it must have been very difficult for her husband and children to hear these words when the time came. (I remember a friend of my mother's who kept telling me she had some home movies of my mother with my son, as a baby, and offering to show them to me after my mother died. I kept making excuses and never did see the film. It was a long time before I could put my mother's picture on my wall, and even today, looking through copies she made of my poor verses in her neat familiar backhand, there is a terrible sadness.)

I was still in Edmonton when Emily died. It was a big, official funeral, with all the town's elite present along with the hearty men of the police force with whom she had loved to work. I had rarely gone to her home that there was not some young girl she had brought from the court "to spend a few days and have some family life, rather than go into detention". I recognized some of them, that day, one slipping up to drop a bunch of blue violets on the coffin.

And I remembered, with anger, two things. One day I was covering a session of the provincial gathering of the local Council of Women, where Judge Murphy was to be luncheon speaker. She had rushed over from court and taken her place, a few minutes late, at the head table, where she gave a rousing speech.

Afterwards, while people were talking with her, a prissy woman came over to me and said with a sneer, "You'd think she'd have taken the trouble to comb her hair and change her stockings." (There was a run.) "After all, this is an important organization."

I simply turned away. When I joined Emily, she whispered, "I hope that no one noticed my stocking and that my hair wasn't too bad. I was detained in court — a mother wanted to talk about her daughter, who was up on a prostitution charge, and she was terribly upset. And if I'd taken time to freshen up, I'd have kept the Council women waiting."

The other incident I still resent came when I was travelling east just after the way had been cleared for the first appointment of a woman to the Senate. On the train was a friend of my father, General William Griesbach, who was a senator. He took me to dinner in the dining car.

"Will Judge Murphy be appointed, as she should be?" I asked.

The stiff-necked old soldier snorted. "Certainly not, if we can help it. She'd make too much trouble — ask too many questions!"

Perhaps Judge Murphy's most active ally was Nellie McClung. They had been very close friends for years. "The McClung kids and Kathleen and I used to play together at one house or the other," Evelyn Murphy told me once, "while our mothers met to work out their strategems in a variety of causes — most especially to raise the status of women." Nellie was a woman of spirit as well as wit and usually handled an audience well. Just to be a woman and have the effrontery to take the public platform could call for criticism and a modicum of buffoonery on the part of a certain male element. (They didn't know them, as we do now, that they were jocks, insecure in their masculinity, etc., etc.) I remember once, however, when the quick, on-target comments the lady usually had for hecklers failed to materialize.

Mrs. McClung was a strong prohibitionist (Mrs. Murphy and Mrs. Parlby were not) and had been invited by the minister at First Baptist Church in Edmonton to follow his sermon one Sunday with some remarks on the subject. As a finale to a well-documented address on the evils of drink, she was in the midst of a vivid and terrifying description of what can happen to the stomach of an habitual drunkard (now it's "alcoholic"). As she concluded, up rose a rather ragged and merry old fellow whose Saturday night revelry had obviously spilled over to the Sabbath. In a loud if somewhat thickened tone he crowed, "I've been drinking whiskey for forty years, and I'll put my stomach against Nellie McClung's any day."

Rising to the occasion, the minister moved forward quickly and suggested, "Let us pray."

I loved Irene Parlby very dearly. She was a gentlewoman in every sense of the word, yet a keen politician. She had soft grey eyes, a beautiful calm face, and never, in my experience, raised her voice. But when she spoke, people listened. Like Emily and Nellie, she had a great gift of humour and a sense of the joy of living, although expressed more in receptivity than projection.

When the Alberta legislature was in session, she lived in a little hotel called the Corona, just around the corner from our home. We often went to the theatre, concerts, and lectures, and, being away from her husband and son in Alix, Alberta, she always gave the hotel a telephone number where she could be reached.

One night we returned from a fine play — *The Barretts of Wimpole Street,* I think — to sit around the fire at my place while my mother made cocoa and joined our conversation. When I called the hotel to give our number, I was told breathlessly, ''Thank God she's safe! The hotel is on fire!''

So we all walked down the lane towards the hotel. Fortunately, the fire was squelched without loss of life or guests' property; it had been a main-floor kitchen blaze. But I think the people there, from bellhop to manager, had been more concerned with Mrs. Parlby's safety than anything else.

There were a remarkable number of first-class women all across the prairies, in the 1920s and '30s, taking major roles in the development of the country and in the problems of humanity in general. I recall especially another close friend, Mrs. Jean Field, a United Farm woman who became an important power in the government, albeit behind the scenes. She too had that sense of vigorous fun and jest characteristic of so many of the pioneers there.

Mrs. Field was one of a committee appointed to pass on sterilization of the mentally retarded, a measure being carried out quietly in Alberta fifty years ago. On the committee was a Roman Catholic priest, a medical doctor, a psychiatrist, and I've forgotten who else. Permission of the retarded in hospitals and/or a close relative was obtained. The procedure meant that such unfortunates could return to the community without producing a number of children they could ill care for.

The program was under the aegis of the Minister of Health, where a man far ahead of his time, George Hoadley, brought in numerous measures in connection with his department. He installed hairdressers in mental hospitals so that women could learn to enjoy looking well-groomed. He established cafeterias, where choice must be exercised and decisions made.

Once while I was at *Chatelaine,* I passed *Maclean's* editor Napier Moore in a hallway. He waved a handful of proof sheets at me. "We're really going to knock them silly with this!" he said gleefully, "Look!"

The heading, in big black type, read: "Should the Mentally Unfit be Sterilized?" The article was written by an eminent psychiatrist.

To Napier's surprise, I laughed. "They've been doing it in Alberta for years," I said. He had had no idea.

Which recalls a time on the *Edmonton Bulletin* when I was responsible for the women's section. I knew that a debate on sterilization was coming up in the Farm Women's convention (this was before the committee was formed). Wanting to get a story, but knowing we were short-staffed, I sent our young society reporter, Jessie Potter, to the meeting. I had earlier dispatched her to report a Woman's Canadian Club speech by then Premier R. B. Bennett, and she had come back with an excellent account. Later she explained that she hadn't understood a word he said, so after lunch this pretty woman waylaid the portly bachelor and explained her predicament; he took her quietly to a corner and patiently repeated and explained the salient points.

Now she turned in her report of the Farm Women's meeting. No word about the sterilization issue. So I asked her if it hadn't come up.

She flushed angrily. "It did indeed," she said, "but if you think I'm going to write about that, you're certainly wrong! Imagine dipping those poor people into boiling water!"

I've know most of the women in Canadian politics, but those Albertans of my early life were very special — I didn't realize how special until I came to eastern Canada to live. As I moved among tea-drinking, white-gloved, twin-sweatered clubwomen and their fragile concerns, I often thought — or would have, if the vernacular had been coined then — "You've a long way to come, baby."

Fourteen

After the war, when my husband changed his Royal Canadian Engineers Officer's uniform for mufti, we bought an old house, as different from the Bennington Heights Drive dream residence as pewter from platinum. It was seventeen feet wide, four storeys high, with a big basement kitchen and a dumbwaiter to pulley food up to the dining-room. Built before central heating, it had a lovely old winding main stairway with mahogany bannisters and posts, three fireplaces, several bedrooms, an attic with a breathtaking view over the city — and one very quaint bathroom. We always did the fun things first (all the luxuries and none of the necessities, as our sons remarked often), and so the top floor was soon transformed into a bar-skyroom, with a wall-to-wall mirror reflecting the cityscape and an extended patio in the treetops with sliding glass doors. We got around to more bathrooms later.

The war was over, we were settling into civilian life, and then came Stanley. Stanley had been the envy of my life when we lived in the modern house over the valley, for he was the English houseman of the wealthy people around the bend. I struggled, coping with three kids and a husband away much of the time on army duty, and I would drool at the sight of the little white-coated man looking after ''his'' family and their children, with tender loving care and good cooking as I can attest from later experience. I saw him often, either when I went to collect my young from play in the big house or when he brought one home around the curve of the ravine. He never let them come alone after dark.

There came a day (we were now in the narrow old house) when I learned, through the kind of coincidental circumstance that so often shapes one's destiny, that he might be leaving his long-time employ. Because he liked us, he came for a pittance compared with what he could have had elsewhere. He became a member of our family until his death of a heart attack twenty-two years later. (Characteristically, even in death he caused no trouble; he simply fell one night while taking his special rice and shrimp casserole out of the oven.)

Stanley took complete charge, and his cooking, like his gardening, became a byword among our guests. We built a sizeable greenhouse, so that he could have his beloved plants all year round. He supplied us with flowers, sustenance, and a deep affection. Mind, we tried him. Many a Saturday morning we could come downstairs after a night of hellering around to find him sitting resignedly on a chair in the hallway, two big shopping bags waiting to be filled at the farmer's market. He didn't drive and often wanted to load the car with produce, including fruit and vegetables in season, to make endless jars of preserves and pickles to keep the budget down. He did much of my personal shopping (time always was a problem) and came home with chuckles about the amazement of clerks when he bought female unmentionables, always in the large size, and they would eye his miniscule stature with some speculation. In his last years, when

"Our man Stanley."

Lotta at sea with her husband, Richard Fisher, in the early 1960s.

the children were gone and we had moved to a small, one-floor house (with big garden and conservatory my husband built) in the suburbs, his life was easier, and he was our good friend and companion. He lived less than a year after my husband, whom he loved and nursed with the tenderness of a mother, and both losses within one year were almost too heartbreaking. I was very grateful for my busy professional life.

The years at Woodlawn West, the funny old house humming with people and activity, were good ones. The lights had come on again all over the world, for what we then thought would be always. I can still see parties with talented friends playing the old piano, set in a nook in the hallway under the stairs, and couples tiered up the winding steps with food or glasses in hand, singing into the small hours. Others clustered in the library, the skyroom, on the patio, in the sun room, talking the great or small talk of the day. Here came reporters, columnists, entertainers, architects, lawyers, judges, doctors . . . all our friends. After two Manhattans, I did a passable sailor's hornpipe. Pierre Berton, with martini stimulant, could barely be restrained from reciting *The Shooting of Dan McGrew*. Joseph Sedgwick, the eminent criminal lawyer and holder of the Order of Canada, was a whiz at Kipling.

I digress here to point out that my hornpiping days came to an abrupt stop not too long ago. I had my small granddaughter to lunch at a family club, and in the dressing-room she asked me to do some steps. I obliged. Back at the office, when I arose from my desk to go home, one leg simply crumpled under me. Astonished fellow staffers called a taxi, piled me in, and, in a wheelchair, I entered Emergency.

"Have you been doing anything unusual?" asked the young intern. I insisted I hadn't; I'd already forgotten the noon demonstration. It wasn't until I was leaving, the leg reactivated with massage and other ministrations, that I recalled my performance. "Oh, I know! It must have been dancing the sailor's hornpipe at lunch." And with that I left.

I always remember, too late, that I should make more explanation than I do.

Many of the strange happenings at our residences came about because of my peculiarly blinkered, child-like habit of following to the letter the dicta of those I respect in authority. For instance, when entrusted with visitations by mental patients, people just released from prison, or others sent to me by supervisory personnel, I never veered from my instructions on how to treat them, no matter how oddly things shaped up. I was not to mention to anyone but my husband that such guests differed in any way from others invited to our home. Of course, we moved in a circle of very catholic tastes, faiths, impossible dreams, and improbable fantasies, and so it was simple to infiltrate my "special cases" into the somewhat erratic course of our normal activities.

Not that there wasn't some confusion due to my rigid adherence to directions. On one occasion a mentally ill young man I had been seeing in hospital was allowed out for a Saturday afternoon (with an attendant) to visit us. We were sitting in the skyroom when one of my sons, now married, came in with his wife. Introductions were made, and the conversation got around to the recent loss of a Toronto reporter and photographer while they were flying with weather scientists in the eye of a hurricane in the United States.

We knew them and were saddened. My son said, "I wonder what the sensation could be, flying in the calm and quiet eye of a raging hurricane?"

My friend from the mental hospital immediately answered. "Very interesting," he said. "I had this odd feeling, when I was there, of sitting in a safe cocoon with all hell swirling around me, a kind of unearthly oasis in a raging sandstorm, being in a still pool with great storm-tossed ocean breakers crashing all around."

My son, fascinated, interjected, "What kind of plane were you in?"

The young man turned to look at him somewhat vaguely. "Oh, I wasn't in a plane," he said.

At this point, my son looked oddly in my direction. Dick hastily suggested a need for ice, and John went off to get it.

Later, when my visitor and his companion had departed, John gave an all-too-familiar shake of his head. "Mum, you and Dad sure do know the kookiest people. Who did he think he was putting on?" Fortunately, at that moment their baby's cry was heard from a bedroom downstairs, and we all jumped to respond. The subject was dropped.

On another occasion we were having the big family Christmas dinner, with those unattached relatives and at-large friends one gathers. Mixed in, unbeknownst to the other guests, were three people recently out of prison. One, after serving on very serious criminal charges, had been designated "habitual"; another had spent five years in the cells after being convicted of some matter of falsified accounts in a big company.

At one point just before dinner, I approached my maiden aunt, a dear old lady, to move her chair from where someone unacquainted with the idiosyncrasies of the old house had placed it — right over the dumbwaiter, which might at any moment ascend at Stanley's push from the kitchen, its shelves laden with turkey and other traditional dishes.

"Dear," she said, pulling me down, "what is a fix?"

I looked at her with slight alarm.

"You know I just heard that charming girl ask the dark-haired man where he got his first fix. And she said something about a detention home, I think. That's what it sounded like. Are they some sort of social workers, dear?"

Fortunately — or unfortunately, depending on how you look at it — at this point Stanley gave the push. Auntie's chair teetered drunkenly, and there was a scramble (not an unprecedented happening at 83 Woodlawn West) to rescue the startled occupant of the instant chair-lift. The fix was forgotten.

I tried, two or three times, to take on people with drug addiction, but found I wasn't qualified. I had this conviction that if one introduced young women who had had unfortunate experiences into the regular flow of law-abiding society, they would rise to the opportunity. I took one such to a well-known private club in Toronto, and we fell in with a lawyer and his wife. The discussion turned to a drug-trafficking case in which he was involved, and he was confounded by my ex-prison friend's acute knowledge and familiarity with all aspects of the problem. I suddenly found the hour was getting late and left almost in mid-sentence, to everyone else's disappointment.

A near-disaster called a halt to any further attempts of mine in this area. A young woman I had befriended invited me to a surprise birthday party for another ex-inmate I had known. She talked excitedly about getting the cake made, candles, wrapping presents, and so on. As it happened, I was kept from attending at the last moment by an assignment at the office. Later I read of their arrests over an exchange of drugs — the police had staked out the party. But for the grace of a city editor in need of a reporter on short notice, I could have been involved.

So I called my friend the matron and asked her to send me, next time, someone without a history of addiction. I asked if she didn't have someone who had had sufficient advantages to be able to fit into normal social situations with intelligent people. I wanted to try an experiment.

She did. Came the familiar password. (When a woman arrived at the office and said, "Mrs. So-and-So sent me," I knew this was a new candidate.) We chatted. She was charming, bright, and eager to become re-established. Her conviction did seem, as she explained it, unduly harsh, and she felt she had been naïve, and thus manipulated. I took her home. She was thoughtful and receptive, and my husband and I began taking her along to all sorts of social events.

Knowledgeable in many fields, she soon made a number of friends.

Indeed, so much so that before my association with her ended, she was offering to introduce me to some of Toronto's most accomplished and wealthiest citizens, who had taken her to their hearts and hearths. That's a long time ago, and I've lost touch. I suspect she's afloat, wherever she is.

Since I travelled a lot, both for the magazine and later newspapers, and had a reckless way of forgetting to mention matters more normal people might consider pertinent (such as inviting a New York literary agent up for the weekend or an Ottawa town planner to spend the night), sometimes there was confusion. My husband, having learned to expect anything or anyone, was rarely fazed — although we did find the literary agent a problem. She had just suffered a broken love affair, and after a party cried her way, rather alcoholically, through the night. This happened to coincide with a period when our baby, not yet a year old, was having long cry-spells to attract attention, also in the wearying hours usually dedicated to sleep. All that night Dick and I met each other going from guest room to nursery, taking turns at comforting the desolate.

Then there was my friend and confrère on *The Globe and Mail*, Fred Thompson. A court reporter, Fred never had acquired the hard-boiled attitude many such assume, even if it is a pretence. He was on the side of the ragged battalions, as I tried to be, and, as his desk was next to mine and we shared a telephone, he often discussed cases with me. (He later was appointed a police magistrate.)

One day an anxious Fred came in to speak to me. He felt he could help an accused man get off if he could keep a certain witness in town. She was a prostitute, he said, and would stay if she could get a job as a waitress. Otherwise she would go to Winnipeg where she had relatives. The waitress job would depend on finding some clothes and comfortable shoes, and she was very low in funds. Naturally, I immediately offered to give her some things and buy shoes. (Nobody should wear another person's shoes, especially in the slugging job of waiting on tables in what would probably be a third-rate beanery.) "I'll bring her around to your place tomorrow at five for fittings," Fred said cheerfully.

What with one thing and another I forgot to mention all this at home. Fred got caught on an assignment, I was held up in an interview, and my unprepared husband answered the door at five the next day. There stood a rather frizzy-looking woman with a strange young man in worn trousers and windbreaker.

Miss D. was expecting them, they said, and Dick, of course, ushered them courteously in. "My name's Boyd," said the young man.

Dick meanwhile was getting drinks. He turned with a laugh and said facetiously, "Not one of the Boyd gang, I don't suppose?" The Boyd gang, the most notorious bank robbers of the day, had been sentenced to prison.

The young man nodded solemnly, taking his Scotch and soda. "Yes, I'm the only one not in jail." He was Edwin Boyd's young brother, Norman.

I arrived shortly after. We had a fine modelling session in my bedroom, the young woman and I, and she left with skirts, tops, and a coat, some rather colourful sun glasses (they were wearing the Dolce Vita types from Italy then) and some of the long earrings that were my trademark. "I think women need pretty things as well as useful ones to feel good," I explained to my husband.

Included in the second-hand wardrobe were some circular skirts then in fashion — one a sweeping deep blue number with a vivid, big peacock embroidered on it. Dick had bought it for me in Rome.

Poor Dick. I guess I had quite a bit of my mother in me at that. He ended by getting a job for young Boyd in construction after some tricky manoeuvring with the union;

ex-convicts then were not really welcomed with open arms. Nor was it the last time Dick threw himself into the breach.

After the Boyd incident, Dick and I were at the Royal York Hotel one night dancing the hours away. Leaving just after midnight, we stood enjoying a lovely starlit evening outside, waiting for our car to be brought around. There was a young woman in sweeping skirts, ornate glasses, and long earrings standing in a somewhat suspiciously stationary but seductive attitude on a nearby corner.

"If you weren't here hanging onto my arm, I'd certainly think that could be you, over by the lampost," Dick said, with keen enjoyment. "I wonder how many of our friends might be similarly misled? You might have given her something a little less distinctively Dempsey."

Fifteen

A regular by-line in a big metropolitan daily is the newsman's version of star billing in the theatre, a brass name-plate for the executive door, or Q.C. appended to the barrister's signature.

It's the top, if reporting is your bag, if you've got those restless scribbler's genes pulling you where the action is as the world spins on its erratic course. Those in any doubt whatever about wanting to be reporters should opt for banking or the civil service. Not everyone is programmed to find lifetime satisfaction in making it to the next edition, all too aware that tomorrow's garbage bag or recycler inexorably devours today's most priceless prose.

My husband and I often discussed the way in which my breed seem always quite prepared to pin our colours to the mist. "You builders will have monuments to your names standing hundreds of years from now," I said (developers and city fathers willing).

"Ah," he would reply, "but what would civilization know of the Parthenon and the Athenaeum if writers hadn't told about them in their day of glory? The recorder of the hour is as important as the long-pull historian — indeed, essential to him."

Be that as it may, gentlemen of the press, either sex, are a curious but readily recognizable offshoot of the race. Involved in the human situation, they still stand apart to watch it function, or malfunction. And since almost every cub reporter carries a foreign correspondent's baton in his knapsack, the risks to life, limb, and any smidge of immortality don't matter. There are hazards, physical and professional. A by-line implies a hell of a lot of responsibility — to readers, editor, publisher, and most especially, oneself. Ground rules call for accuracy, honesty, digging, and often waiting (God, how you wait, sometimes, closing in on a story) and as astute a piecing together of odd-fitting fragments as employed by any first-rate detective. And there are always the open manholes — such as the danger of shaping information to conform to preconceptions of your own (or an ever-ready press agent or publicist) or the temptation to skimp on checking *all* sides of a story.

Top men and women I've known in the business have a kind of plus quality, like great athletes and performers. It's almost a precognition, or intuitive sensitivity, especially to the false or phoney. All this, with a terrier tenacity in pursuit of fact, adds up to what has long been called, for want of a better term, a nose for news.

There'll be no star dressing-room or autograph seekers among your confrères in the city room, that storied environ of news sleuths. It's as down-to-earth as a construction site. Common practice, when a fine reporter is just back from an important, perhaps even dangerous, assignment, is to make casual chatter at the water-cooler. The returning native's by-line may have been spread over the front page for days, date-lined Vietnam or Brazil, the high Arctic or the lower

Volga. Usual greeting is, "Haven't seen you around. Flu? Holidays?"

When I came to *The Toronto Star,* it was the big time for me in my field. Despite years on other dailies and in various communications media, this was action central. I was not young. Could I meet the challenge?

I had become bored with the slower pace (in those days, anyway) of *The Globe and Mail* and felt I was in something of a rut, however comfortable and pleasant a daily-column rut could be. As so often before, I felt it was time to move on. The *Star*'s reputation (and indeed, practice — I had experienced it often in opposition) was to staff all the big stories competently, everywhere. It intrigued me. I had grown up, more or less, on the *Journal* and the *Bulletin.* The *Globe,* then, as the only morning newspaper in the big city was something of a law unto itself. The *Star* and *The Toronto Telegram,* an imaginative and lively publication, fought fiercely for the lush evening trade and reader attention. Both had absolutely top-bracket editorial staffs and the competition was zestful and electric. (The *Telegram* has since ceased publication).

The *Globe* had, I later felt, a peculiarly insular philosophy for much of my time on staff. It considered itself the "literate" daily, *The New York Times* of Canada, pursuing its own ends in a kind of well mannered jog-trot. As a managing editor once explained to me, there wasn't what you would call a *Globe* story, but there certainly was a *Globe* approach. Much of this has changed with the advent of the bright and aggressive *Toronto* (morning) *Sun* and its saucy, sometimes brassy, impact on the downtown crowd.

Coming to the *Star,* I felt a little as I had done when, paddling down the great quiet Peace River in a fire-ranger's canoe, we came suddenly to the swirling white water of the rapids. Would my frail bark withstand the pressures? I arrived to report to senior editor Borden Spears, who had hired me, feeling very much a wee cowering beastie.

My first lesson was a telling one. A weekly feature I had done at the *Globe* for many years was called "The Cleaning Lady". I based my character on Annie, a Ukrainian woman who had been my mother's much loved weekly helper in Edmonton. I knew her pronunciation, her solid goodness, her down-to-earth judgement, and her wisdom. Now, with capable maids and other household staff dwindling to a handful tussled over by the rich, the weekly cleaning woman was a common denominator among urban householders. Needless to say, my "Annie" always outwitted the lady or the man of the house (not to mention the children). The one-upmanship was always in her favour, and her stories of other employers she served poked fun at the person worked for, never the employee.

The feature had had a wide following, especially among women who read their morning paper over a second cup of coffee after the rest of the family had gone. (Today, the women are usually off, too.) So the *Star* asked me to carry on with it. In no time, I was getting angry letters from cleaning women and their families for downgrading honest labour and imitating funny accents. We were just entering into the solemn era of human rights awareness; there was just no room for humour involving people anxious to protect not only their rights, but also their dignity. (Perhaps that will change when people can finally relax, secure in the knowledge that they have the respect they deserve.) Furthermore, I found, *everyone* read the *Star*. I stopped the series permanently.

My second awakening at the *Star* came during a period, fortunately brief, when due to some alterations columnists were working on a floor far from the city room. (I disliked the isolation and suspect that is why my newspaper had banished me part-time of late to a lonely place to write this book — so I'd get done as quickly as possible.) I telephoned my boss to say I'd be out of town for a few days, but was leaving columns to cover the interim.

Borden Spears asked, in his gentle and courteous way, if it would be an impertinence to inquire where I might be going.

"Not at all," I said cheerily. "There's a free-load flight and weekend in Nassau. They're opening a new hotel, and I'll just be gone three or four days."

Mr. Spears then wondered if I would mind dropping down to his office. He explained that the *Star* did not allow free-loads (jaunts on which press people get passage, board, and room gratis and usually other pleasant perks of various kinds).

I was astonished. I hadn't known that, I said.

Then he went on kindly, "But if you want to go to Nassau, or anywhere else, and you see a legitimate story for this paper and will give me a memo on it, we will assess the project and, if acceptable, pay your way."

Most of the big dailies, including *The Globe and Mail*, no longer accept such favours. But in my earlier newspaper days I always had a railway pass on the two Canadian transcontinental trains and once had taken a month's cruise in the West Indies paying steerage fare and being accommodated in such first-class quarters that I could barely keep up with The Quality, or the tips. This despite the fact that my wardrobe had been expanded mightily by the best summer outfits of two or three girlfriends.

Free-loading still is a matter of concern where it is condoned. I soon came to see the wisdom of the *Star*'s long-held policy. If it comes to the crunch, in reporting a hotel or railway or airplane or big company story, perhaps a disaster, even the most scrupulous reporter finds it more difficult to bite the hand that has fed, wined, dined, bedded, and transported him, if that be necessary.

But the *Star* was as good as Spears's word. In fact, I soon learned that memos I was accustomed to write to managing editors in dreamy contemplation of stories far away were read and answered quickly, usually in the positive. I had been accustomed to waste-basket treatment for many of my brain waves. Still, one of the best trips of my career wasn't even my idea. And I blew it.

It was January 1961, and I was now in the full steam of front-line reportage for the *Star*. That meant being one of the home-office people appended to our Washington bureau for the inauguration of President John Kennedy. It was a high, bright period in American affairs, and the literate, handsome son of a glittering family was the toast of Canada as well as his own country. His beautiful, dark-haired young wife Jacqueline was a breathless interest as well, both at home and abroad. Along with all the protocol, ceremony, solemnity, and hoopla of the most important national ritual in a great democracy, this occasion had a heightened vitality.

The large, energetic Kennedy clan had connections and associations from Whitehall to Hollywood, from Harvard to the black ghettoes. A brave new day was dawning, and the capital was in fine and revved-up spirit.

Patricia Kennedy was then married to film star Peter Lawford, and stars of stage, screen, and television swarmed in for the event in unprecedented numbers. Lawford was a member of Frank Sinatra's storied "rat pack", and never before nor since, in my experience, have the greasepaint brigade had so much to do with affairs of state. (There were moments when Sinatra seemed to be running at least a part of the off-stage action.) The receptions and parties were a glamorous mix of celebrities of the day in almost every field. You'd see Adlai Stevenson, defeated presidential candidate, deep in conversation with Jack Paar, then at his peak as a late-night TV showman and Sammy Davis, Jr. locked in talk with Ethel Kennedy.

The Stephen Smiths — she was Jean Kennedy — gave a late-night party after the big day's ceremonials and receptions, and I stood outside in the freezing January night watching the thirty-fifth president of the United States arrive in a swirl of film stars, all as easily recognized and as heartily cheered as the man who was to guide the country through its coming perilous years. As always, when I could in Washington, I huddled with the White House press corps, who were generous in pointing out the people I didn't know, along with comment. President Kennedy had had the reputation of being quite a ladies' man before his marriage, and so there were many interesting people to be observed and described.

Earlier in the day, I had made my first surprising (to me) assessment of Jackie Kennedy. It was entirely unexpected, when I had arrived as full of admiration and ready acclaim as any heroine-worshipping American for the slender, beautifully dressed woman. Like her countrymen, I had a warm appreciation of the fact that this well-born and educated first lady, bookish, lover of the arts, and as much at home in Europe as her native land, was of a very different temperament from the sports-oriented, rollicking, extroverted Kennedys. An orchid in a field of tiger lilies, perhaps? A fragile tropical fish thrown into a tank of playful porpoises?

That day at the inauguration, I just didn't like her at all, yet I found the Kennedy sisters great — friendly, communicative . . . well, democratic. I was so surprised at my reaction that it took me years to confirm what had been almost intuition then.

True, the outdoor inauguration ceremonies took place on a bitterly cold day. Still I was surprised that the young wife of the president, whom people had come miles to see, spent as much time away from the big flag-bedecked stand as on it. (There was a retiring room built inside so that those involved in the ceremony could come and go.)

But my feeling had more to do with the distaste Mrs. Kennedy appeared to feel for the "undisciplined" parts of the parade, in which children and various adult groups cavorted, danced, and played along. She always seemed to emerge for the stylized, spick-and-span military bands and regimental marches-past. Of course, the high-spirited garb and demeanour of some of the civilian groups was not of high style or cultural impress. But hell, this was everybody's day, and it was a celebration as well as a time of solemnity. The "amateur" displays didn't seem out of place to me in such a diverse and many-faceted nation. Nor did it seem ludicrous to contrast them to the awe I felt as a frail, old, white-haired man came forward and recited, almost inaudibly, President Kennedy's favourite poem, with the lines, "For I have promises to keep, and miles to go before I sleep." The garishly dressed celebrants from Nashville, or wherever, were as much a part of America as was that beautiful old man — poet Robert Frost on his last public appearance.

I brushed much of my feeling aside and wrote none of it. Mrs. Kennedy was not a robust woman and, indeed, the day was cold. But I was to see that slight curl of lip, the widened nostrils, and the look of distaste again. And I was to confirm any feelings I then had had much later on the day of Bobby Kennedy's funeral at Arlington Cemetery. I'll talk about it later.

You can see that the Kennedy inauguration, with the running, observing, writing, filing, and the weather conditions, made for a full several days and nights. When I at last finished my assignment and returned to New York more dead than alive, I checked into the Algonquin Hotel. No room at that inn — but I knew from of old a little closet-like room in staff quarters. I could usually bed down on the cot there in an emergency. I dropped into it, very late.

At four in the morning the telephone rang. Drugged with weariness, I answered. It was the *Star* night editor from Toronto. The voice seemed a million miles away.

"There's been a ship pirated out of São Paulo by its captain. Jack Brehl's left from here, and we've got a booking on the plane for you at LaGuardia. He'll meet you there."

"Where's São Paulo?" I asked dimly.

"South America, of course," came the voice again. "The ship, the *Santa Maria*, is somewhere out in the Atlantic, and they're out looking for her."

I was almost too tired to speak. "Look," I said, "I've got very poor eyesight, and I haven't had any sleep for a week. I just can't get up now and make a plane in two hours."

There was a pause. What I had said was tantamount to mutiny, but I went on. "I'm sure Harry Hindemarsh (then managing editor and grandson of the *Star*'s founder, Joseph Atkinson) wouldn't expect you to send me now."

I could almost see the shrug. "I'll phone him myself," I said.

It was four o'clock in the morning, but I called Harry. He was shocked that I would be so inhumanely treated when I had turned in so much copy over the past week. "Go back to sleep, Lotie," he said. "This is inexcusable! I'll certainly tell that night editor off!"

Wearily, I resumed my slumbers. With eight hours rest, of course, I began to regret my haste. But newspapering is a fast-paced operation, as I knew, and already others would have been given this exciting assignment.

When I returned to the office, I met the night editor at the water cooler. "Guess Harry Hindemarsh had some strong words for you about cruelty to the lower order of beasts," I said, with little satisfaction now.

He grinned and leaned over the faucet. "Yeah. It was Harry who'd called us to send you."

Sixteen

What's he really like? For the first time in history, millions of Canadians, along with astonishingly large numbers of other people around the world, were asking that about a Canadian head of state. They'd been asking it from the day in 1968 when Pierre Elliot Trudeau became the closest thing to an instant prime minister this country has experienced.

I've enjoyed considerable opportunity to study the visible Trudeau, an enigmatic, almost mystic lawyer-intellectual, the unknown who materialized full-blown on the Canadian consciousness and into global view like a neon-lighted astronaut suddenly limned against an arid moonscape. Ottawa, the Canadian capital, *was* considered pretty arid territory, not to mention ho-hum Yawnsville on the Rideau, by the country at large — that is, by those beyond its exclusive power brokerage. And the rest of the world? Well, everybody who knew about Prime Minister Lester B. (Mike) Pearson's Nobel Prize admired him, in a living history-book kind of way; those of us who were in personal contact with

Mike loved him and his ready congeniality and warmth. As P.M., John Diefenbaker was the epitome of the Canadian Abe Lincoln — the fighting prairie lawyer who could stand up to entrenched interests in Bay Street and St. James, where the stock marketeers of Toronto and Montreal weave their invidious nets. He had no international following, any more than did R.B. Bennett, Mackenzie King, or "Uncle" Louis St. Laurent, other Canadian prime ministers I have known.

But never, in travels over my own country and abroad, have I had so many people of every stance and station ask, with such genuine curiosity, "What's Pierre Trudeau really like?" Is he a playboy iconoclast? A connoisseur of beautiful women? That was the earliest picture. What had taken the dashing Montrealer, independently wealthy, with the blood of both French and English Canada in his veins, fluently (and naturally) bilingual, into the bear pit of politics?

To his early life as a privileged son of wealthy parents, with opportunity for all the best in education and cultural advantages, Trudeau himself added the mix of hippy-ing, if you like, around the world, living with people of the lowest estate from Mexico to India. But he lacks one important ingredient for the image of a successful politician; never was Trudeau, nor will he ever be, an easy first-namer or your friendly neighbourhood good Joe. He's the born and cultivated patrician, a thinker and planner in the Jesuit tradition, with ill-concealed scorn for what he considers stupidity or for encroachment on his private life. More than that, he lacks the ability for ordinary person-to-person communication on any intuitive basis.

He has a kind of protective shyness, a need to keep some inner core from contamination by the vulgarities of the insensible. While he can communicate readily with those of his own intellectual and cultural status and with simple or disadvantaged people without pretences, he is most lost with what we might define as the great mass of the middle class.

So why would this very powerful segment of Canadian society take him to their bosom at election time, spell his name in letters ten feet tall across the ballot boxes of the country, and mob him like a superstar of sports or entertainment whenever he appeared? What turned on cautious, middle-of-the road, self-effacing Canadians, often considered colourless, in a frenzy of adulation so sweeping and uncharacteristic that it became known, deservedly, as Trudeaumania? Far easier to understand what turned them off when, as must to all men and women, came realization of weaknesses as well as strengths, human frailty along with magnetism and high skills in the art of living and being alive. But what (which really is the miracle of leadership of Pierre Elliot Trudeau) accounts for the residual support he still holds, now that the first fine careless rapture has simmered down, support on which to build a solid re-election base, twice over?

My observation is that both Trudeau and the nation matured. We were in a mood for celebration, an emotional surge of late-blooming sense of nationhood after centennial year, 1967. Even the most Francophobic elements across the country had been affected by the magnificent Expo '67 in Montreal. The world had come to see us, to be our guest, and we had a new and, sadly, fleeting sense of unity. It was time again for a French Canadian prime minister (just as we rotate French and English Canadians as governors-general), and this man seemed to represent the best of our two founding bloodstreams and cultures. He had, along with very great erudition, a sense of gaiety and nose-thumbing at pretension and stodginess, and we wistfully hoped some might rub off on the rest of us. Then, too, he was our first real find as a television natural in the echelons of higher politics. Television, as Richard Nixon once learned to his sorrow, is a telling tool in the structuring of a leadership image.

All this is, I think, a valid assessment, because I am not a Trudeau man (woman? person?) *per se*. His dislike of the print press is well-known, frequently expressed, and often patently unfair. Trudeau has been accused, and justly, of arrogance. But that is passing. He is an admitted pragmatist.

"For a long time he didn't care or want to bother about the political underpinnings, the framework and nitty gritty of politicking," I was told by one of the men closest to him, one in great measure responsible for his education in this direction (which almost came too late, as Trudeau picked himself up after near-defeat in his second election and did his homework carefully enough to ride to victory in the third). "There was a time when he would give his famous shrug (very French Canadian), and it wasn't until that close call he began to realize, I think as much to his own surprise as anything, that he *did* care, did want to lead the country, did want to be a politician, if he must, as well as a statesman. He cares now, believe me. He's completely involved."

There's no question of Trudeau's integrity. We've been unbelievably lucky in this respect in Canada. Robert Stanfield, leader of the Progressive Conservative opposition, and David Lewis, now deposed leader of the New Democratic Party, are men of the most unchallenged integrity. We have yet in this decade to witness dirty tricks in our national party leadership. And our plumbers, though outrageously over-paid, stick to their pipes and drains.

Editors of *The Toronto Star* were convinced (when many people were not) that this reluctant Canadian, who had been, indeed, drafted by a power group in the Liberal party (many of them English Canadians outside Quebec), would be chosen leader of his party. In our system, since the former leader Mike Pearson had announced his retirement (for reasons of ill-health), the new party leader would automatically become prime minister until an election.

Robert McKenzie, head of the *Star*'s Paris bureau and a former prize-winning Quebec reporter, was brought back to Canada to cover Trudeau's campaign for the Liberal leadership and to do research on the still little-known man who had risen rapidly from parliamentary secretary to the prime minister to justice minister in Pearson's cabinet. I was sent to Ottawa from Toronto to join Bob and, under his direction, share in the research. The assignment came suddenly, as most such do when senior editors make a decision, and I was on my way with nothing more concrete to work on than a portable typewriter, notebook, and pencils. So I had ten days in Ottawa and Montreal (a rare luxury as time goes in the newspaper world) to dig into all I could discover about Trudeau's personal life.

"Where do you start?" I've often been asked by would-be journalists. Well, Trudeau was a Montrealer, and so I registered at a hotel there. I'm a great believer in libraries, particularly newspaper libraries, followed by the use of the telephone book. But Pierre Elliott Trudeau had so far achieved sparse space in library files. His home telephone number was unlisted, and I was able to get but one tenuous lead. It was Bob Giguère, chief Liberal organizer for Quebec and a personal friend and backer of Trudeau.

Then, as so often and so amazingly happens, luck was a lady. With a little legitimate hanky-panky at Liberal headquarters (like being an old friend and party worker from Toronto who had misplaced dear Bob's address), I was on my way.

A beautiful young brunette answered the apartment buzzer and, although obviously reluctant, allowed me to come in. It was Giguère's daughter, Diane, there for an hour to take some of her possessions to a new apartment she had rented on another floor. She had known Trudeau since she was 13 (she was now 30) and, after a few preliminaries, generously made coffee while we talked. By the time I left the very talented and articulate young woman, a novelist and announcer on the CBC French network, and, luckily for me, fluent in English, I was well briefed on a man she greatly admired, with book and verse about his family and some interesting insights into his character.

I found other young intellectuals in his circle then, girls he had taken out, and, because of the *Star*'s perspicacity in hitting the trail early, I was able to get to his very elusive brother and pleasant but publicity-shy sister before the hordes descended. The family soon withdrew from press contact. I also began to piece together a clear picture of the woman who had undoubtedly had the strongest influence on Trudeau's life.

She was his mother, the former Grace Elliott who had a Scottish father and a French Canadian mother. Thanks to her English schooling at college, she spoke that language beautifully and used it with the children at home. Thus they grew up completely bilingual. His father Charles-Emile Trudeau was the son of a French Canadian farmer who, although he became a lawyer, soon turned to business and made the family fortune. Pierre was only 14 when his father died, and while the two brothers and sister were compatibly fond of each other, it was Trudeau's closeness to his mother, an intelligent, quietly strong woman, which marked his life deeply in the years until her long illness and death, at 82, in 1973. Friends tell of receptions and dinners at the big family house in Outremont, where intellectuals of all age groups would meet and mix, while Trudeau shared the hosting with his mother. He was deeply devoted to her, and theirs was an intellectual friendship and companionship as well as filial-maternal relationship.

Woman friends found him charming, a sympathetic listener, a gay and stimulating escort (he is an excellent dancer), but elusive when it came to deeper levels of emotional involvement. "He was always as precise as a time clock, meticulous in everything he did, at work or play," said one long-time friend who asked not to be identified. "It is this very meticulousness and application that is his greatest fault. He has built his life on systems of ideas, abstractions. He has never committed himself to anything . . . not until now, at least."

And Diane Giguère noted, "He can close in like a shell, put up a wall. He is no playboy. He doesn't like waste of people or things."

Another woman who knew him in his younger days said, "You would always find these intense young intellectuals around him. You never felt you had his exclusive attention."

Trudeau's older brother and sister are both shy and private people, and I felt when talking with them they were quite astonished at this new direction in the mercurial brother upon whose own privacy they would never think of impinging. It's that kind of family. "He'll be a good prime minister. He's always been successful at anything he put his mind to," his sister Suzette (Madame Pierre Rouleau, who married a dentist) told me. "And he'll stay at it unless he gets bored."

There are some small facets of Trudeau's character I learned then, from his brother and sister and a number of friends and associates, that seemed unimportant at the time, but now I think indicated later developments — particularly his choice of so young a woman for his wife and the ups and downs of Margaret's temperament, much publicized later.

His sister told me he rarely remembered, or in any event marked, family birthdays or other such events with gifts. "Instead, he'll find something rare or lovely in his travels and send it along anytime." (Acceptable behaviour in a bachelor, but not always where a wife is concerned.)

His in-laws, the Vancouver Sinclairs, were a close-knit family with a big, hospitable house and a busy but pleasantly informal social life revolving around the several daughters. Occasions like birthdays were important, and the kind of guarded privacy the Trudeaus observed among themselves would be of a very foreign nature to the Sinclairs. And Margaret was their youngest, and so rather special.

"Not that she was coddled," says a close friend who often visited, "and she had been off on her own, you know, working in Ottawa. But there always was a very outgoing, easy warmth and communication.''

Yet Trudeau was such a private man even close friends, like Montreal publisher Jacques Hébert, with whom he visited China (they wrote a book about that venture), spoke of his many experiences in which Trudeau would have some separate ventures and never mention their content. They would just come up, accidentally, one way or another. Hébert also spoke of Trudeau's strong faith as a Roman Catholic, which did not preclude wide and open interest in other faiths, including Buddhism. (Margaret changed her religion when they married.)

Especially, I think now of something his sister and Hébert both told me — of his interest in the young. ''Trudeau is at his best with children,'' Hébert said. I have since observed that many times, following him on campaign or other trips. Once I was coming down a stairway in the Edmonton City Hall, where he had just signed the guest book. Outside, hundreds crowded around to greet him, many of them children. Trudeau had been given an Edmonton signature hat — the tall gray topper so many of that city's people and visitors wear during the annual celebration of Klondike Days, an old-time western fiesta. It is as indigenous as the Calgary Stampede's cowboy wide-brimmer. U Thant, then secretary-general of the United Nations, was in Edmonton at the same time to receive an honorary degree at the University of Alberta with Trudeau. I watched the dignified Oriental take no pains to disguise his dislike of such frivolous headgear and immediately lay it aside. Trudeau donned his and, as he came down the stairs and glimpsed the people waiting through a big window, turned back to an aide, beside whom I was walking.

''Have I got it at the right angle?'' he said, seriously, tipping the hat to a cake-walk stance. How vain, I thought. Then, after the aide nodded, Trudeau added, ''The children expect it to be right, and I don't want to disappoint them.'' It was a genuine concern, and I never saw him play the cheap political trick of kissing a strange baby . . . unless it was a she and anywhere from teens to seventies.

Something else Trudeau's sister told me made his choice as a wife a girl who could have been his daughter (twenty-nine years younger) make more sense than the theories put forward by a lot of people. I reported in the *Star* at the time of my interview with her:

> An unusual facet of Trudeau the teen-ager was his interest in younger children.
>
> She (Trudeau's sister) remembers they used to come to the door to ask him out to play. An example was the friendship of Pierre, then 16, with Philippe de Gaspé Beaubien, who was only 6 years old. (Beaubien was director of operations at Expo '67.)

And his brother Charles, an architect (whom I reached only because I mentioned my husband had been an architect), spoke of Pierre's fighting instinct as a young boy. His toughness and combativeness, traits mentioned by many friends, have often been displayed in Parliament and on other occasions; fortunately, he now uses a sharp and cutting tongue, rather than fists, to bring home a point.

So here you have an enormously complex man, considered the catch of his own country, if not well beyond, marrying a young and obviously adoring woman from a very different milieu. (Margaret is erroneously thought by many people to have been exposed in the political fishbowl because her father was a long-time Liberal politician and for five years minister of fisheries in the St. Laurent government. All that was while she was a very young child, only three when he joined the cabinet.)

Trudeau is not the only bachelor who, playing the field until middle age, finds his true love in a beautiful young woman and prepares to settle into serene domesticity. But what have we here?

Those first months and years (as I write, the Trudeaus have been married only five, with three children), I watched Margaret Trudeau in Ottawa and elsewhere, apparently the perfect image of what Trudeau and the world at large expected — retiring behind the shadow of her husband in public, being clucked over by the veteran parliamentary wives of Ottawa (a sometimes intimidating bunch), and shepherded through the rituals of openings and official receptions and dinners by some such kindly mother figure as Paul Martin's wife. I recall one occasion when I sat close by them in the private gallery of the House of Commons, and Mrs. Martin, behind discreetly sheltering fingertips, whispered a whole Who's Who of information.

Margaret's pretty face seemed of the placid type, and to all appearances, she was fitting beautifully into the expected role of young wife and mother, always perfectly dressed for state occasions, charmingly casual, even hoydenish, when out of the spotlight. There were many endearing scenes, because the Trudeaus usually took their baby, even when very small, along to parties; Margaret would leave the gathering to go to the bedroom and nurse her child. Then would follow the clutch of adoring older women (mostly, they were) to admire Justin or Sasha.

But somewhere along the line, we began to get a noticeable touch of personal women's lib at 24 Sussex Drive. There was an unexpected and enormously frank and open interview, laid on quite suddenly, with a *Star* reporter. It was so unabashedly unguarded and honest that shock waves spread through the capital and into the far hinterlands of Newfoundland and Vancouver Island. Then, as unexpectedly, Margaret accepted the invitation of the head of a Japanese shipping line (which had reason to seek good relations with this country, because of business here) to launch a new cargo ship. Mrs. Trudeau also accepted the gift of costly camera equipment and announced she planned to study photography.

Her secretary called Doris Anderson, editor-in-chief of *Chatelaine* in Toronto, offering Mrs. Trudeau's services as a free-lance columnist. Doris told me later she naturally accepted with pleasure. (Margaret could have written sections of the telephone book and, if well illustrated with family portraits and a few ad libs, it would have brought curious readers.) From Japan, Mrs. Trudeau then announced her intention of writing the column, somewhat precipitously, since no further negotiations had been made. There was some critical press, and Mrs. Trudeau announced she would *not* write a column. Doris told me she was then refused access to Mrs. T. by telephone or letter. (A number of letters and wires I have sent seeking interviews have never been acknowledged, and this perhaps has happened to others. Yet every time I have approached Trudeau himself, during a chance encounter, about doing a story on the new regime at the official residence, he has been charmingly acquiescent. "Just write my office," he has said. I have. No response.)

Then Mrs. Trudeau sought psychiatric help — again, much publicized — for a brief period. At various times, she has talked of her hope for the day when she can live a normal life, do her own housework, have her husband free of such heavy national and international responsibilities. (Not a really punchy prelude to any upcoming election for a candidate.) So what's with Margaret Trudeau? In some of the unexpected turns she has made off the beaten path in the tortuous jungles of high politics, I think I see growing pains of protest, such as I once noted exhibited by a much younger Prince Philip. There must be a time when that two steps to the rear of a spouse (metaphorically, in Margaret's case) can be irksome.

It was Philip and Princess Elizabeth's first visit to Canada, and they were at a big VIP luncheon in Vancouver. Not yet long married, Philip had been accustomed to the decorum with which press and public were kept from access to royalty in Europe. He was finding it different in Canada. A Canadian tour co-ordinator visiting the Royals in London before their visit told me Philip had suggested pool coverage of events — that is, token representatives of the biggest members of the media would be assigned to coverage, then pass along or "pool" their reports to the rest. While this could be done at times, as at very formal dinners, receptions, etc., the Canadian explained patiently that it just wouldn't be accepted in North America for a whole tour.

At the luncheon Princess Elizabeth had spoken of events scheduled in the very formal format ahead. Philip, in loud and well-heard tones, announced to his immediate tablemates that he planned instead to go fishing by airplane with some newly met Vancouver magnates. The Princess's face, usually well under control on any occasion, was all too expressive of her surprise and displeasure. But Philip went. It was a little childish, but a protest against too much subservience, which, I think, did establish the beginning of his independence in many ways. He has since moved around the globe on his own pursuits in a way no British consort ever did before him.

So Margaret Trudeau may very well have been establishing some sort of right to do her own thing. And her husband began, from what one heard, to reassess a relationship which, while obviously loving and mutually respectful, could take too much for granted. The world was not unfolding as it should according to the way Trudeau had always planned and organized. I think he took a new look at the pretty young woman he had married. So we come back to, what's Trudeau really like?

He's governing in a period with world conditions so precarious, inflation such a problem, environmental control — indeed, the condition for future habitation on this earth so in question — that it is unfair to blame him for the distemper of his time in his own country. His courage is unquestioned,

137

and he learns from mistakes as well as unexpected drifts in human progress or regression. It is doubtful if an English Canadian prime minister could have handled the delicate, often perilous French fact in this country as he has, frequently on ice so thin that the torrents of nationalism, both French and English, often seem about to inundate the nation.

He has a very deep and gut love of Canada, and I have heard him at his most impressive and poetic when he speaks of the great beauty and richness of the land — forest and mountain and river — all of which he knows as few of his countrymen do. And he has learned that in statesmanship as in canoeing, co-operation is sometimes a better choice than individual showmanship or achievement.

Trudeau had done a lot of canoeing in the relatively safe and navigable waters of Algonquin Park. When he joined an expedition 450 miles long in the barren lands, from the source of the Coppermine River to the shores of the polar sea, he soon discovered teamwork was essential. Fellow travellers Eric Morse and Angus Scott told me that it didn't take long for Trudeau to replace some early displays of derring-do with the split-second co-operative paddling needed to traverse the icy waters, deep canyons, and swift rapids of that northern waterway. And he shared chores of cooking and camping with meticulous care — sometimes, as Scott told me, with hands split from the cold water and covered in bandages.

"But he still had this sense of privacy, of a reserve you did not try to break through, even on a remote campsite far from civilization."

My own conclusion is that no one really knows all the parts of this very complicated man. Perhaps no one ever will. It will be interesting to see how the only person equipped to unveil the real Pierre Elliott Trudeau will handle that chore when the time comes. But I doubt that even the inevitable autobiography will really pierce the mystery.

Who was the artist who wrote, "I would paint what's in the bottom of my heart, if I could see that far"?

Seventeen

Bea Lillie, the incomparable Canadian-born but really very British comedienne (she went to live in London early and married Lord Peel), once found herself a weekend guest of cosmetic queen Elizabeth Arden (also Canadian born). This was at Miss Arden's palatial country place in Summerville, South Carolina.

After a wearying plane flight, La Lillie wakened Sunday morning to drink in the amazing breadth and depth, fittings and furnishings, of her bedroom suite. It was all very, very pink (Arden's favourite colour in both packaging and fashion), and the beauty products that were the basis of the small-town druggist's daughter's fabulous fortune were everywhere on display.

Bea made her way to an ornate desk, found it well stocked with postcards picturing the Arden domain, and wrote to actor Murray Matheson in her bold, wide-eyed scrawl: "Dear Murray, will you kindly tell me exactly what I am doing here?"

Throughout my long life in the press, I've echoed that thought so many times it's engraved a kind of permanent question mark in my response mechanism. Not to mention that of others so dim-witted as to become involved with me in one way and another.

"Exactly what are you doing *there*?" It's a question asked me by managing editors, radio and television producers, magazine executives, comptrollers of assorted expense-account operations who thought they were in control, and concerned relatives — at all sorts of times, in all manner of places.

Often my peregrinations had that sort of flavour of Eydie Gormé's lovely song line, "You start for the corner and end up in Spain." "What are you doing in Rome?" an editor once cabled, after I had filed a story about elections there. (I had last been sighted touring France's Fountainebleau Palace.) Or, "What's this request from the United States Air Force to allow you to fly an experimental jet at Lougheed's California base? You're supposed to be in Hollywood inter-viewing movie stars." Or, "Have you had shots?" when I reported from a leper colony in British Guyana, supposedly on a meandering travel cruise of the West Indies. I always turned in the assignment first, but then I frequently found time and opportunity on my hands, and who's to waste those precious underpinnings of the life experience?

I thought about it when I was doing a legitimate assign-ment interviewing Bea Lillie, and she laughed at the mention of her card. She had come to New York to play in entre-preneur Billy Rose's *Seven Lively Arts*. But that was the only time I could make her smile in the long dressing-room session we had between acts of her sparkling performance.

She had just lost her only son, and she was a little lost herself. It was wartime, and the relative remoteness and life-as-usual atmosphere in the United States was difficult for her to assimilate at this time. Bea had been on duty in several areas of military operation and spoke of how it had been, performing from the deck of a British war vessel for thousands of fighting men, somewhere in African waters, and scheduled for assault manoeuvres the next day.

"They were so young, so eager to respond when you tried to entertain and amuse them — and for so many it would be a final performance."

She told me that all she could do to ease the pain of everything that was happening, of all she had seen and felt, was to walk. "I walk miles and miles," she said. "The other day I started out to work off pressures and forgot I had no money for a cab back. Not even for a telephone call. So I walked back. I was pretty tired for the performance that night."

I never got to Elizabeth Arden's country palace, but I did interview the wiry little beautician several times, witnessing in the process some of her petulant behaviour. You judge.

Once, in her Fifth Avenue Salon in New York, she told me about a manager of part of her world-wide chain of operations in Australia. "She was a bright, very able woman," Arden said, the icy blue eyes glinting, "and I asked if she would like to come to our New York headquarters. She was quite excited and soon arrived. She was fine in the salon. But my dear! I invited her to the country for a weekend and discovered the woman couldn't play bridge! We had a foursome all lined up. You can imagine my embarrassment!" Later the woman quietly decamped back to Australia and, one suspects, less strictured after-hours employment.

When Arden was scheduled for a visit to the big, plushy salon in the Robert Simpson Company's downtown store in Toronto, the advance alert and drill preceding her arrival was akin to that for an admiral touring an off-shore base. She expected every operator and salesperson to do his or her duty faultlessly. That included one manager I know who always had to go away to recuperate after one of these confrontations. He may just have been especially vulnerable; there were those who said the favoured ones were treated very generously.

I was reminded of one time I visited *Time* magazine's news bureau in Paris. Clare Boothe Luce, wife of *Time*'s publisher Henry Luce, was quite a woman. Not only a brilliant playwright (and later American ambassador to Rome), she was also a far from behind-the-scenes power in *Time-Life* policies and patterns. Along the wall of one side of the central room of the bureau was a big blackboard marked out calendar-fashion for the month's assignments and activities involving various members of the staff. For one whole week upcoming, all names and other vital statistics had been brushed out. Scrawled simply in big letters across that time sheet were the capitalized words "MRS. LUCE HERE".

But back to Elizabeth Arden. In Toronto she liked to stay at the beautiful residence of the late president of Simpson's, Edgar Burton, and his charming wife Clayton, a former reporter. Edgar was a decisive magnate, having taken over the reins from his father, Charlie Burton, in the big department store chain. He was well accustomed to the wear and tear of big business. But on at least one occasion, when I went to his home to interview Elizabeth Arden, he was indisposed with a sudden case of influenza. Clayton had to do the honours solo.

At that time Simpson's had the exclusive rights in Toronto to an Arden salon, and the Canadian manager was summoned to the Burtons', on a Saturday, for conference with Miss Arden. He was just leaving as I arrived. His face was flushed, and Mrs. Burton looked uncomfortable.

"What do you mean, I can't go the Royal Winter Fair on Sunday? That's the only time I have, and I want to see the horses," the beauty queen declared imperiously. The manager tried to explain patiently that the Royal Winter Fair was not open to visitors on the Sabbath. "Well, then get it open," she ordered. Clayton tried to explain that it just couldn't be done and finally the conversations were concluded in a hallway, out of earshot.

So we started our interview on that note. Miss Arden was all business now, and Mrs. Burton left us alone. At one point, as I was writing in my notebook, Miss Arden gasped. "My dear," she said, "look at those hands!"

I looked — mine, needless to say, were the ones under disapproving inspection. While they had been well scrubbed, there was no question that a little tender loving care might have erased years of pencil and typewriter pushing, both arduous finger exercises leaving certain tell-tale crinkles and even, I'll admit, a callous on the pencil-bracing third right finger.

"First," she said, "use Elizabeth Arden Hand Cream. It works wonderfully on my horses' legs." "Then," she continued, reverting to every inch the beauty-palour operator she once had been, "wherever you are, whenever you have time, just rub your hands together, like this." She demonstrated with the motion one might use in washing painstakingly or, since it was done more slowly and forcefully, the gesture one observes in people suffering physical or mental anguish — that of hand-wringing.

Next morning, while waiting at a bus stop for a transfer change, I recalled the advice and, never to disregard a free prescription from a high-priced source, began the treatment. I felt a touch on my shoulder. "Is there anything I can do?" asked a kindly gentleman waiting in the line-up behind me. "You seem in some distress. The way you're wringing your hands," he said. "If I can help . . . ."

The horsey-leg look didn't appeal to me either, and so I cut short the course.

One of the strangest off-beat and off-schedule events I got into was in London, where all sorts of lovely and unexpected things can happen, if you let yourself be involved in some of the idiosyncrasies of that village on the Thames. For it still is a village, in many ways, never having regimented (as though London would want to) its millions into goose-stepping automatons. I use "goose" in the barnyard sense, not the military connotation.

I had been on assignment in London for *The Globe and Mail* and conned them into letting me stay over several weeks and do my daily column from there. By the time my husband arrived for the final fortnight, I was up to my typewriter roller in any number of things.

I had found a native photographer to work with, and his enthusiasm for his overseas assignments could only equal mine in my discovery of so much of his town. The people at the hotel desk had become accustomed to this cheerful, rushing, and usually untidy type roaring in on urgent business and let him come up to knock on my door at any time.

The morning after my husband arrived in my hotel room, there was a knock at the door. I had had little opportunity so far to tell him of my doings, being so eager to learn all the news of home and hearth. When he answered the door a dishevelled figure waving a sheaf of photographs rushed by him, leaned over the side of the bed he just had vacated, and said excitedly to its nightgowned occupant, "Coo! Look what we got in the latest bunch!"

My husband coughed politely as he closed the door and rather stiffly drew attention to who he was and to the fact that he was here. My friend leapt up, shook hands heartily, welcomed him with great gusto, and showed him the photographs.

"What we're doing," I said when Dick suggested some leisurely sightseeing the next day, "is much more important. We're going to save the Third Programme and the St. James's Theatre."

"Just the two of us, strangers at that?" my spouse asked mildly. He had been catapulted into so many ventures at such short notice that the projects came as no news — just the rather ambitious nature of these particular endeavours.

"Of course not!" I said. "I went to this meeting with the barrister and his friends at the Inner Temple and they've got a two-prong thing going and it's very exciting. We're going to march from St. Martin's in the Fields tomorrow morning at eleven, right to the St. James's Theatre, and hold a protest meeting. They're talking of tearing it down, you know, and putting up an office building. As for the Third Programme . . . ."

Dick broke in, "I know the Third Programme on the B.B.C., baby. It's the classical music and other arts one. I did read at home there was talk of cutting it out. Would it be too great an invasion of privacy, or secrecy, or whatever, to ask who the other friends are?"

I explained I just didn't have time to go into that. But they were awfully nice and I was sure he'd like them and, as a matter or fact, we were having a meeting this very afternoon to finalize arrangements at Ralph Vaughan Williams's.

"He's in it. You know, the English composer."

Dick did indeed know well, for his knowledge of music was vastly deeper than mine. Vaughan Williams was then an old man, and that very night was to be guest of honour at a program of his work by the London Symphony at beautiful Festival Hall.

"Anyone else I might know?" he asked, now enthusiastic.

"Oh, yes. There's Laurence Olivier and his wife, Vivien Leigh. And Christopher Fry, the playwright and poet. They're all delightful and so dedicated."

Dick mused a moment. "I know I'm stupid, but I can't help finding myself wondering just how you got into this?"

I said, impatiently, "That's terribly simple. There was a letter in the *Times* by the barrister, and so I went to see him." That, of course, explained it in terms any child could understand. "And there'll be all sorts of artists and actors and musicians and people in the march," I went on, "like these nice girls I met backstage at the play in the Majestic the other night. They want me to bring you around to the show."

The march was great fun, along the streets of London, just like a procession of royalty, with the bobbies waving us on.

Olivier and Vivien Leigh led us off, and we all climbed a fence at a construction site opposite the St. James's and sat on high planks while the leaders talked to the crowds.

But I think Dick most liked the afternoon at Vaughan Williams's lovely "grace and favour" house, one of the residences Britain provides for very distinguished citizens who might not be able to afford, especially in declining years, the surroundings they have so well earned through contributing to the joy or welfare of their countrymen.

Dick and the composer struck up an immediate accord. The Briton was very old now, with an ear trumpet and confined to a wheelchair. Dick sat, literally, at his feet, and very gently, when the old man whispered to him, wheeled him out and attended to him in the washroom. Then Vaughan Williams took him around the drawing-room, pointing out his favourite things (I was deep in a huddle with the organizers of the march), and Dick always remembered with especial tenderness the little statue of the Pipes of Pan on the grand piano.

I met Sir Laurence years later in the little Blue Bar of the Algonquin Hotel in New York. This day, Dick had gone to see an ophthalmologist, having contracted an eye irritation. "I'll be too anxious to wait in the hotel room, dear," I said, worriedly. "I'll just sit in the lobby until you come back, and so I'll be right there."

When my loving mate returned, fortunately with the problem solved, he says he saw three rather rowdy tipplers around a table, laughing and talking and gesturing. One was his terribly worried wife. The second was Herbert Whittaker, drama critic for *The Globe and Mail*. The third was Sir Laurence, who had been with Herbie when I came along. As Dick appeared, feeling somewhat the intruder, Olivier was saying, "Just call me Larry, Lotie." We had already gone over the day of the protest march. When I spoke of how movingly that lovely actress, Vivien Leigh, had spoken about St. James's, he nodded. "She's quite the old girl, my wife."

Indeed she was. And the manhattans being what they are at the Algonquin, I wrapped up the meeting in its proper dried rose petals and have never addressed one of the greatest actors on the English stage — indeed, in the world — as Larry, or anything else, again. I've seen him many times on stage since then, but haven't attempted to contact him. That was an adventure whose time had come . . . and gone.

Eighteen

What about sex?

I thought you'd never ask, although, as a writer born into an age when we customarily undressed indoors and with blinds drawn, I'd be tempted to paraphase Prime Minister Trudeau's remark that the government has no business in the bedrooms of the nation. Has the reader, in a more or less autobiographical book, keyhole privileges to the boudoir? Only, I suggest, when that area has been spelled out as shared accommodation in the terms of purchase. On the other hand, if you'd care to join me in Professor Alfred C. Kinsey's Institute for Sex Research, the grand-daddy of them all, we'll set the scene.

It was springtime at Indiana University, and the beautiful greensward of the campus was dotted with flowering shrubs and trees and a strewage of students. You had the impression that the college was not only co-educational in and out of class, but also that the first contemporarily scientific insight

149

into the sexual life of human beings had cast its glow at home as well as abroad.

It was the early 1950s, and Dr. Kinsey had just shattered whatever remnants of Victorian prudery still clung to the hush-hush subject with his weighty and academic report, *Sexual Behavior in the Human Male*. He was now completing research on what surely could be called a sister volume, *Sexual Behavior in the Human Female*.

I'd talked with several men who had co-operated with Dr. Kinsey and knew him, including my brother-in-law, the late Professor Gordon Brown, an anthropologist. The consensus was that the researcher was a fine scholar and highly respected zoologist and that his book on women would be as revealing and myth-shattering as the one on men. Despite the world-wide furor and accusations of prurience (the first volume had been banned in some countries), it was a fine and greatly needed study in an area shrouded in the mists of ignorance and misconception.

So I suggested to both *The Globe and Mail* and *Chatelaine* magazine that I visit Dr. Kinsey and his research staff to do stories in advance of the publication of the book on women. (I had just left *Chatelaine*, under amiable conditions, to do a daily column in the *Globe*. The arrangement was satisfactory.)

When I wrote Dr. Kinsey, I got a reply offering to see me, but under certain conditions. He knew both publications I would be representing and that was fine. But I must agree to take the lengthy test for the sex case histories — an invariable rule where writers of articles on these works of his were concerned. In addition, I had to be prepared to spend several days with him and his associates, so as to understand thoroughly what they were about and why. Kinsey was a highly regarded scientist and didn't want any half-baked assessments or uneducated guesses about his important work.

Naturally, I agreed to the terms. In return, he courteously arranged for me to stay in a special visiting professors' residence on campus; mine was a lovely but simply decorated suite done in early American pine. Indiana is beautiful at this time of year; the campus was then spacious and magnificently bucolic, and I thoroughly enjoyed the whole week, mixing with students when I wasn't working and enjoying the honour museum, which contained, among other mementoes, some of the writing of the famed World War II correspondent, Ernie Pyle, a graduate.

Dr. Kinsey was a big man, physically as well as academically, with a shock of white hair and keen blue eyes. He was very popular with students as well as staff, as I observed one day when we strolled around the campus licking ice cream cones he had bought at a corner tuck shop. He had a fine sense of humour and with some glee showed me several scrapbooks he had of scathing reports, editorials, and comments on his "male" sex book. It's difficult to realize in this permissive sexually open day the furor caused by his research and findings a quarter-century ago. He hadn't bothered to thus assemble the complimentary reports, a number of which I had seen in the press.

We had several sessions, in which he explained the whole basis upon which his work had been started. He emphasized that he was purely a researcher, not an analyst.

A world authority on wasps, particularly the ball wasp, Dr. Kinsey had been teaching undergraduates in zoology in his easy, informal way. "I began to realize, when I was discussing sexual practices in the insect world, that many of my students knew very little about the whole subject," he said. "So I found myself answering more and more questions about sex, especially relating to humans." Then a group of male students came to him after class one day to ask if he would hold some sessions with them on the whole matter, particularly where it related to themselves. From those out-of-school gatherings came his appreciation of the need to compile scientific data on sex habits of humans, and he started with the male.

"It was very interesting," he said, "how sexual practices in the male world fell into readily recognizable patterns when assessed in the light of education, literacy, and cultural opportunity. For instance, there was marked similarity in the habits of males who were university graduates, members of the learned and other professions — much more preparation and sex play and participation of the female in a leisurely way.

"Among unskilled workers and those with few cultural advantages, the sex act often was much more direct and physical. In fact, many of the men we worked with on interviews and questionnaires in this group indicated they felt sex play somehow dirty, demeaning."

It was one of Dr. Kinsey's associates, a younger man, who divulged the difference in findings where women were concerned. (Dr. Kinsey didn't discuss it because the book was not yet completed, but over a few beers, the younger man told me. I had been commenting on the "patterns" found in male sex behaviour.)

"Funny about women," this man said. "I'm out on the interview teams, and we expected something of the same thing as with the men. To our astonishment, it just didn't hold at all. You could go through a factory, say, interviewing women working on very similar routine jobs. Or to a college sorority house, where many very well-to-do daughters of affluent families lived. Or apartments or houses in a middle-class neighbourhood. There was just no pattern. Every woman was different in her approach, her response, to sex."

Well, came the day when Dr. Kinsey, the great man himself, was to spend three hours taking my history. It had been part of the bargain.

He explained first, "We have three sets of tests, which ask the same questions and aim at the same factual information, in different phraseology. One, for those of little education; second, for the man and woman of high-school education; third, for the well educated."

I couldn't pass up the implied compliment when he began asking me questions with words of three and four syllables I had never heard in my life. Several times I hesitated, scrambling frantically through my mind for clues in Latin or Greek prefixes or suffixes. At one point he enquired if I had ever practised something with a name so long and involved it made no sense to me whatever. As I paused, wondering if I should tell him I hadn't a notion in hell what he meant, he said soothingly, "Don't worry." He patted my hand, a little gingerly I thought. "We've had two cases of this in our research. One in Australia and one in mountain country in Arkansas.

I made a stab at several others. I was in too deep now to retreat. Furthermore, I didn't want to lose my story; I was afraid he'd decide I didn't have the intellectual background to report lucidly on his work.

"Yes," he said, at another time, "uncommon, but not unknown."

When we finished, he looked at me rather quizzically with something of a smile. I don't think I really fooled him at all, but he added, "This is going to be one of our most interesting case histories."

I suspect, even in today's terms, that that questionnaire is either filed among those of the world's kinkiest deviates — or is used to indicate to researchers how they can detect the flounderings of a simple creature over her depth and refusing to admit it.

For my remaining hours at the centre I slunk around shamefacedly, but the staff was friendly and willing to go out for coffee or a beer as always; and I wasn't ousted from my pleasant lodgings. But I do remember one thing. Just as I was saying goodbyes and thank-yous, I saw Dr. Kinsey disappear into his office and loitered to talk to his secretary, a very pert and wise woman.

"You know," she said, as I was telling her how much I appreciated all Dr. Kinsey's patience and kindness, "we all love Prok (as they called Professor Kinsey) and most of us have been with him for years. I was here when the offices were full of ball wasp specimens and they seemed pretty ordinary compared with some of the characters we see around here now." She poured me a final cup of coffee out of the perculator, then went on. "Prok says there's no such thing as abnormal. But for my money, there are an awful lot of queer normals wandering around."

I never could tell whether my case history was one included in the book on females. All I can say is, echoing Dr. Kinsey's secretary, there were an awful lot of very odd normals wandering around in the pages. I well may have been among them . . . very much a stranger to myself.

Second only to my reputation in Dr. Kinsey's case history file is my probably very tattered one with a woman in London, if she's still around, who was a desk clerk at the Cumberland Hotel at Marble Arch.

Ken MacTaggart, Bruce West, and I, then columnists and staffers at *The Globe and Mail*, had been sent to London for the coronation of Queen Elizabeth II. Bruce arrived early to do "atmosphere" stories. Kenny and I came on a later plane, At the airport, Bruce met us very excited about the beauty of London, preening herself with flags, lights, flowers, and lavish street decorations of all kinds to mark this great event. "We'll check you in quickly," he said, "and then you must come out and see London by moonlight. We may never get another night like this." (He was right. It rained steadily afterwards.)

So when we got to the hotel, Kenny said, "You register and Bruce and I will gather up the luggage so that we can get out as soon as possible." It was now close to midnight.

I went to the desk, and what appeared a very proper and stiff-lipped English lady handed me cards. "You have reservations for Miss Dempsey and Mr. MacTaggart from Toronto, Canada," I said, pleasantly, "and we asked for three adjoining rooms. I'd like to be in the middle, if possible." She looked not only disapproving but also astounded. I'm not really the sexy type, and both gentlemen looked highly respectable. So I thought further explanation was forthcoming and, as Ken and Bruce were telling me to hurry up, I added, "You see, we have to have access to each other at all hours of the day and night; me, especially with both of them."

This was quite true, as always with a "team" of writers from one newspaper working on an out-of-town assignment. Time is of the essence, and there is need to report areas or events covered or unusual news items discovered, so that we wouldn't overwrite one another. This was expected at home base, as the speed with which copy must be moved might mean different editors would handle individual stories. I grabbed the keys, we threw our things in the rooms, and we were out and about London town.

Throughout my stay in London the proper Englishwoman at the Cumberland Hotel kept a rather wary eye on me, nodding without smiling whenever I came to get my key. We were on close to a 24-hour routine, and I took time out only to call my husband in Toronto and beg him to get over in time for Coronation Day. He had been planning to join me afterwards, and we were going to Italy and France on holiday. "You must come," I said. "It's just something you've got to share. I've never seen anything so exciting or so beautiful. Flowers are arriving from countries around the world and the streets are like great gardens, and the lights and decorations, and the people . . . ."

He got the last seat on the last plane out of Toronto, bringing, as requested, some "stay awake" pills by prescription from our doctor. None of us on the *Globe* team was accustomed to taking anything like this; but we had decided the pressures of work, especially as the big day drew near, might require special medication to keep us on our toes.

As usual, I had forgotten one small item — to mention to the woman at the desk that I was married or that my married name was Fisher. On news jobs I always register as Miss Dempsey to save confusion when calls are being returned and for the home office making contact. I had also neglected to mention that my husband would be arriving to share my room. The one in the middle.

As so often happened, Dick arrived to check in, and there was no answer in my room. So he simply explained, "My name is Fisher. I'll be sharing Miss Dempsey's room." Now the woman was really shaken to her marrow. As I say, she hadn't considered me the ménage-à-trois type, but a foursome?

Dick sighed, explained the situation, and finally achieved access.

None of this fazed Madge. Madge was our chambermaid, and we all had come to love her dearly. She mothered us and accepted these "Canydians" as her special brood. Each morning she brought tea and other breakfast vitals to our beds, without knocking. We opened our eyes to her gentle shake and blinds being raised. The morning she found Dick there, she shook him gently too, greeted him warmly, then went away to bring back another tray.

Coronation morning Kenny and I were to be in the Abbey, Bruce out on the streets with the people. We had to be up at five, and so I had gone to bed fairly early for once. Dick had joined Bruce in a colour-finding night prowl around the streets, now thronged with singing, happy people settling in to sleep or chat the hours away.

I wakened at about 3.00 a.m. No Dick. So I gathered my robe around me (my hair in curlers) and sleepily walked down the one flight of stairs to the big hotel lobby which, like so many in London, was also a bar. Everything was wide open this night and morning and there I saw my light of love and Bruce merrily drinking beer with a couple of young ladies whom they were, both explained later, interviewing.

"I don't know about you, Bruce West," I said, "That's Ada's problem (his marvellous wife). But Richard, up to bed, m'lad."

At five o'clock Dick was running from my room to Kenny's, getting Kenny into his required full-dress suit, then back to zip up my long gown. I had forgotten head covering, *de rigeur* for the Abbey ceremonies, and Dick was about to go off to try to find me a hat or scarf in one of the shops.

But Mayor Charlotte Whitton of Ottawa offered to lend me a beautiful silk scarf she had been given by the Begum of something or other. (She was in full mayoral robes, splendid ones she had designed herself, with tricorn hat and chains of office.)

"You should learn to be a lady like Charlotte," Dick said, returning with the scarf. "She carefully explained to the floor attendant what was happening and left the door to her suite wide open all the time."

Coronation night, after all our stories were in, Dick and I were invited to a special celebration supper being given by Torontonians Viola and George MacMillan at the Trocadero. (The MacMillans were then big shots in the mining world, Viola being the first woman president of the Canadian Prospectors and Developers Association. She later, unfortunately, was called upon to serve a jail term for some financial misdemeanours in the stock market.)

The stay-awake pills had been just great. I was going strong. But, being a neophyte in this department, I didn't know there could be a sudden reaction when the effect wore off. This happened to come at the height of the celebration; my head dropped suddenly into a plate of chicken surrounded with vegetables and gravy. I vaguely recall Viola noting this was a shame, because the affair had cost her $15 a plate (a high price in those days) and my loving and understanding team-mate practically carried me out and into a cab.

We were leaving for Paris a day later, and Madge came in with breakfast. She was sorry to see us go. "Why don't you just stay here, loves?" she said. "What could be finer than London? Besides, you'll find nothing but foreigners over there. A lot of them can't even speak English."

In Paris, we laughed over two previous experiences I had had in the Georges V when I had been there unhusbanded and less sophisticated.

I had been writing a series of columns from Europe and sending them home by airmail to Bob Farquharson, managing editor of *The Globe and Mail*. They were chatty and impressionistic, rather than hard news. I numbered each column, as I did my carbons. When I got back and went through the issues in which they had appeared, I noted that column number eleven seemed to have missed publication.

"Didn't you get my column about the different types of salons available to businessmen from abroad?" I asked Bob. "I thought it was quite interesting."

I had noted a pleasant-looking woman in the lobby of the Georges V, chatting with different men. It was an expensive and well-known hotel, and I was curious as to what she was discussing when she approached them. I thought she must be some kind of Y.W.C.A.-type secretary, giving information about sightseeing and points of interest. But on approaching her I found her reticent; she merely smiled, shrugged, and turned away.

I then went up to a couple of nice-looking men who had been talking to her and asked if they spoke English. They did. So, always one to nail down a story, I asked what they had been discussing with the lady.

They smiled. "She tells you about the different types of social life you can find here," one said, "if you know what I mean. There are charming ladies in Paris who will welcome you, and it's a matter of price and just what sort of entertainment you are seeking." And he went on to explain the fee structure and *divertissements* available.

I thought this a valuable insight into the City of Light, since I had not observed anything of its sort in Canadian hotels of this class, and sent along a story.

Bob snorted. "Can you imagine the angry horde of wives of Canadian businessmen who would have descended on us if I'd run that very detailed book, chapter, and verse of prostitution in the higher echelons for future guidance?" he asked. Well, you can only try.

The other Paris experience we laughed about was one in which an American fellow reporter, with whom I had come in contact on some news sleuthing, offered to come to my room and give me more data. I eagerly accepted his kindness — this has been common practice at home. To my surprise, I learned he had another sort of co-operative effort in mind, and after a slight scuffle, persisting to the door, he fled, somewhat dishevelled. Just at this moment a little French chambermaid came around the corner. She followed me into the room. The bed with its big frilly pillows and soft pink eiderdown had been carefully turned down on both sides.

She walked over, turned one side of the bed back up, and looked at me with sympathetic warmth. "Too bad, Madame," she said.

It didn't occur to me until later that she thought I had been making the overtures, with obvious lack of success.

Nineteen

Reporting isn't all fun and games. Or even adventure and travel, performance, and parade — or getting to know some of the people the world is curious about. Many of the big stories deal with tragedy and disaster — accident, flood, fire, mob violence; the grey underbelly of life on this planet — poverty, suicide, mental or physical illness, human suffering. War, and the aftermath of war, crime and jails, and the beached wreckage of individual lives.

"The world is a comedy to those who think, a tragedy to those who feel." Most of us strive to maintain the delicate balance between logic and sensitivity. Good reporters get all the facts. Great ones, in my experience, develop such empathy with the people, places, and things involved in a story that they bring happenings alive with words that, as Kipling once remarked, "walk up and down in the hearts of all their hearers".

Yet some part of the newsman must stand aside, weighing, assessing, absorbing, then recording — all usually at very great speed and under clocked pressure while the whole tenuous human situation seems to be breaking away in small pieces.

Looking back, I wouldn't have missed one of even the most soul-searing moments of the catastrophic events I've followed. People tend to become very basic, very simple, in time of great trial. All the subterfuges, the pretences, the vanities, and the vainglories melt away in the white heat of gut experience, whether they stand or run.

As a reporter, I feel the public must know, must be aware of even the saddest or most sordid happenings that affect us all. I learned long ago in my father's grocery store how one bad orange at the bottom of the crate can spread its fungi and decay to the top, often unseen unless there is constant vigilance. I am very proud of the part my trade has played in letting people *know*, even at personal danger or to much abuse.

"I don't want to be involved." "It's so depressing." "Why don't you just write about pleasant things?" "Life's too short to get into the murky scenes." My own feeling is that a lot of head-in-sand ostriches get their tail feathers clipped — or come up for air too late to find any left uncontaminated.

I've watched a good many brave and courageous people fight their way through ignorance and prejudice, usually on behalf of those unable to fight for themselves. They got involved, and they've won new deals for the aged, the handicapped, the retarded, former prisoners, neglected children. And they seem to undergo some distillation of spirit in themselves — a continuing unfolding of and strength in the verities. A shining example is Pauline Vanier, widow of one-time Governor-General Georges Vanier. Madame Vanier, through the years I knew her in diplomatic life, was a warm and beautiful woman. Today, since her devotion to and absorption in the magnificent work of her son, Dr. Jean Vanier, with retarded adults around the world, she has such a glowing quality it emits a kind of glory. If anyone has "put her hand in the hand of God" it is Pauline Vanier, and enough has rubbed off that I cannot be in her presence without a sense of tremendous humility.

Yet she has never lost her feeling of joy in life or her quick and ready laughter. I remember in particular a family-type dinner at Daybreak, the residence for adult retarded in Richmond Hill, Ontario. I asked her if she had ever in her entire life found it possible to be rude to any human being.

She thought, then nodded. "Once," she said, with a grin as close to wicked as she could muster. "My husband and I were asked to entertain a Toronto businessman and his wife at dinner in London. That was when Georges was Canadian High Commissioner there. Our guest was an insensitive and abrupt man and at one point turned to me to say, 'Madame Vanier, do they understand your French in Paris?' "

I should explain here that Pauline Vanier was born in French Canada and educated there and in France. There has long been discussion over whether the French spoken by those of limited education born to the language in Canada is different, in many respects, from that in the mother country. The implication was insulting. One of this woman's cultural background would be as much at home in the Sorbonne as a well-educated English Canadian would be in Oxford or Cambridge.

"So," she continued, "I just smiled at my English Canadian countryman and said, sweetly, "As well as they understand your English in London, I fancy."

When I think of the Vanier breed and their sublimation of personal loss and sadness in going out to serve the needs of others, I recall poet Stephen Phillips's words with new understanding: "Out of our sorrow have we made this world so beautiful."

Memory is a curious collector. Perhaps when we are in the grip of terror or agony or wounds beyond belief, the situation becomes so overwhelming that we find ourselves caught up by the fragments that *are* within our comprehension. Why do I see still so clearly I would know him in a crowd of thousands the old black man lying with his head against a tombstone at Bobby Kennedy's funeral?

Great funerals, which are as awesome as any of man's ceremonials, have a strong core of unity. I've covered a number, including those of Premiers Maurice Duplessis and Daniel Johnson of Quebec. I remember simple people filing past the ornate open caskets, many lifting small children to look on the waxen face of death. And long lines of Very Important People in silk hats, walking slowly in processional along sun-sweated streets. And the local politician, at Duplessis's funeral, coming behind me in the long line of those paying respects to the terrible little dictator of his province, pressing something into my hand. It was an Eversharpe pencil with his name on it. "See you at election time," he said with a wink.

The assassination of the attorney-general of the United States, following so closely on the terrible murder of his brother, President John Kennedy, sent shock waves around the world. Not only did Bobby Kennedy's burial bring the great, the near great, and thousands of just ordinary people to Arlington Cemetery that day. Not only did it remind all of us, as death of friend or stranger does, that our own last drum roll is sounding from some distant hill. This violent ending to the life of a national figure, coming after the assassinations of the president and the great black leader, Dr. Martin Luther King, also brought home to Americans an ominous feeling that they could be entering a period of violence in their history unknown to peacetime in that freedom-loving land. It hung like a pall over the air in what seemed endless acres of graves in that cemetery — so many of them simply and similarly marked for men who had died in battle.

I had covered the pomp and ceremony of the lying-in-state of Kennedy's body in St. Patrick's Cathedral in New York City. Then I flew to Washington for the final rites of burial.

Jack Brehl, a fellow reporter on the *Star*, was covering the train journey from New York to Washington with the casket, the Kennedy family and high-ranking mourners, and a section of the press corps. I was to do a story on the graveside service. Bobby Kennedy's press secretary, almost as though too stunned to realize this was the last event in his employer's career for which he would shepherd reporters, organized us and our arrangements were made — accreditation badges; baggage taken care of; press buses at hand; food, drinks, and lodging meticulously arranged.

On that hot and murky day I arrived at the cemetery, in company with a large group of fellow scribes, to find crowds already gathering. What none of us could have foreseen, of course, was that the funeral train would be held up by an accident. Crowds swarmed all along the route from New York to close in on the slow-moving train. At Elizabeth, New Jersey, an express travelling the other way ploughed into throngs on the track, killing two and injuring five others. This added tragedy meant many hours under a relentless sun in a place not designed for long vigil.

There was no place to sit or eat, and the only two washrooms were in very poor condition and very dirty. As Washington bigwigs began to arrive, they found it necessary to line up with the many poor and grubbily attired people pouring into the cemetery. Their faces revealed that for many it was a new and highly distasteful experience. And they did look funny — smart Washington women in couturier clothes and men in formal funeral attire, threaded among the long line of "the others" of varying sizes, shapes, and colours, and cheerful in what was long accustomed indoctrination in waiting in turn, even to go to the toilet.

Many a well-massaged bottom conditioned to delicately patterned and colour-co-ordinated bathroom tissue that day bore the print of a page from the crumpled old magazines thoughtfully supplied by someone when the regular toilet rolls had run out. (I was reminded of my Eaton catalogue days in the outdoor privy of the farmhouse where I stayed when teaching school in rural Alberta.)

I had plenty of time, as it evolved, to wander over the area and down a grassy slope to the enclosure in which Kennedy was to be buried, near the grave of his brother, John, where a flame was kept burning. VIPs were allowed down around the fences there; the rest of the crowd spread over the hilly slopes that formed a kind of amphitheatre. I traced the path the funeral party was to take up and down the hillside and examined the gravesite. The fence around these special graves formed a square, with gates in the middle of each side.

Then I found a spot on the grassy hillside where I could view the proceedings and watch the Kennedy family — still held up by the accident. As I usually did in a foreign country, I stayed close to one of the biggest news agencies native to the place — in this case the big trucks of the National Broadcasting Company. Not only would I be able to hear their newsmen and watch the direction of their cameras, but I also found, as so often, they were getting direct news from home office of value to me. They also were kind enough to share soft drinks and sandwiches, not available anywhere else I could observe.

So there was this old black man, lying in the sweltering sun with his head on a tombstone. His son was trying to persuade him to leave, aware that the wait was going to be much longer than anticipated. He shook his white head stubbornly. "I go home when Bobby come home," he said softly. And he stayed, into the eerie moonlight that made such a surrealistic picture of the thousands of tombstones stretching into the horizon. For as night came on the harsh floodlights of the television cameras and interior lights of the studio-trucks were the only other illumination.

Finally the Kennedys arrived, and soon the whole moving and sorrowful service was over. Ethel Kennedy and her children were beginning to form a line for the slow walk back up the hill. The cameramen were packing their equipment.

Suddenly there was an electric pause, and I saw the TV technicians rushing to get their gear back in working order.

Jackie Kennedy, with her then young children, had moved from the recessional and, with one on each hand, was walking around the back of the fence. I noticed then that Caroline and John each had a tiny bunch of white flowers in their hands. Ethel and her family were obviously startled. This was not in the arrangements.

The president's widow moved around three sides of the fence (although there were open gates through which she might have entered) to walk across, past her brother-in-law's new grave, to that of her husband, which was in direct view of the television cameras. This gave everyone time to set up again and to catch the little ceremony in which each of the children stopped and placed flowers on their father's grave. My American news comrades were shocked.

"I think," one of them said, slowly, "it may be a Roman Catholic custom to bring flowers to your own dear one's grave whenever you are in the cemetery."

A cameraman snorted. "Not for this one, bub. She just couldn't allow Ethel to have even this moment without taking the spotlight."

Not long after I was at a party at Frank Shuster's (of Wayne and Shuster). Harold Town, internationally known Canadian artist (and writer par excellence), came over to me.

"I was reading your stories about the Bobby Kennedy funeral," he said. "You don't like Jackie Kennedy, do you?"

I was astounded. I had made not one comment or critical note about her performance.

"No, I don't," I replied, "but I certainly didn't say so in the *Star* stories."

"No," Harold said, smiling, "you let her hang herself."

Yes, memory is curious collector. My most vivid recollection of the terrible damage done to life and property by

Hurricane Hazel, on October 15, 1954, was of a little emergency-help centre quickly set up the morning after in a church basement in Etobicoke. One whole street and all its houses had been washed away. A woman with uncombed hair and staring eyes wandered in, hugging an alley cat so tightly that it was shrieking. Someone tried gently to take it from her arms and brought her tea. The cat was all she had left of her house and husband and children from that awful night. Somehow, miraculously, she had stumbled out. And back in the office, I remember seeing a big, strong guy, one of our top photographers, with tears in his eyes when the first edition came out. His photograph, taken that terrible night from a high tree, hadn't come out. He had nearly been killed, but the tears were the tears of all of us who have risked and somehow, through no fault of our own, missed fire.

I had been to many banquets and other festivities in the great old Royal York Hotel, once the biggest in the British Empire (it may yet be, as to number of guests rooms). So the morning after the terrible *Noronic* fire, September 17, 1949, it was strange to visit it as a morgue. Of a holiday shipload of tourists, many from the United States on a few days' cruise, a large number had lost their lives when late at night the boat went up in a burst of flames while tied to the Toronto dock. A Royal York banquet room was turned into an emergency morgue, and here came suddenly summoned relatives from across the border to try to identify their kin.

The picture engraved most vividly on my mind was of a tall young man, going wildly from sheeted slab to slab, pulling back covers. I came over sympathetically, and he opened his hand. In it was a charred human finger, and on the finger was a wedding ring. ''That's my mother's,'' he said. ''I'd know it anywhere.'' He had found it among the smoking black timbers of the boat.

Sometimes a tiny paragraph in a newspaper sets you off on a sad and sorry journey, as one from the *Star* sent me to a town called Dresden, Ontario. I read it and couldn't get it out of my mind. It was a request from the chief of police there that anyone having information about Judy Yott, a missing 13-year-old girl, report to him. What bothered me was that she had been missing for some weeks, and this was the first I had heard or seen of it.

I asked for a few days to go to Dresden and did. The police chief, Alvin Watson, was not pleased at my interest. "I finally put that in because the mother was after me," he said. "I suspect she's just got in a car with some fellows and gone off." He indicated that the family was not too well thought of; the mother was a rather strange widow who "boarded" children. Well, the Boy Scouts were going to go out one Saturday and search some of the countryside, but it rained, he said. And he turned away to something else.

So I started to follow the trail of little Judy in March of 1960. Her adoptive mother, Mrs. Margaret Yott, was indeed strange. There were some grown sons, and this little one had been adopted when the people who left her in the woman's care as a baby never came back. (Adoption laws were not as stringent then as now.)

Mrs. Yott showed me an attic full of dolls she had collected. She fondled them. I saw the little girl's bedroom, where a crib at the foot of her bed contained a Mongoloid child, a boarder. The child, who appeared to be about two, was unable to do anything for itself. "Judy was very kind and helpful," the woman said.

I asked about her school, a doctor she might have seen, any friends. I learned that Judy sometimes visited a neighbour and her husband. They had no children. "But she hadn't gone there the last little while," the mother said. At school I discovered from the teacher that Judy had been a quiet child, of ordinary intelligence, no trouble. The doctor was similarly not very helpful. So I went to see Judy's friend.

She turned out to be a very religious woman with a very neat and proper house. Yes, she had had the child in, had combed her hair, cleaned her up, tried to help her learn to be a good person. She felt sorry for her, and as far as she knew, she was Judy's only friend. "But I had to stop her coming," she said.

What had happened, I learned with growing horror, was that Judy had told this righteous woman that she was going to Toronto to the Canadian National Exhibition, to stay with relatives. "I knew the child had no known relatives and that she wasn't going to the Exhibition," her "friend" said, "so I told her she was lying, and I couldn't have a liar coming to my house."

Chilled to my marrow, I thanked her and went back to the chief of police. It was March, still snowy and cold. I wanted to know when and where Judy had last been seen. By now the police chief was very annoyed (news travels fast in a town of 3000 people, and I had also gone to see the weekly newspaper editor).

He sullenly took me to the police station door and pointed to a hall a few yards away. "Someone saw her standing in the doorway of that hall around eight o'clock at night," he said. "I told you. A lot of cars go through here."

I went to the doorway and looked around. I could clearly picture that lonely miserable child whose one friend had branded her a liar when she had woven a few so-needed fantasies in her small and lonely heart. I was convinced she had simply crawled away somewhere and lain down, rather than go back to the idiot child and strange mother.

So I came home and wrote a story called "The Town That Didn't Care". I predicted Judy's body would be found somewhere in the area, somewhere she could walk to and just lie down.

Chief Watson was on the telephone immediately to my editor. He was going to sue. But luck, Judy's hapless luck, was with me. A few days later, before he had initiated legal action, Judy's little frozen body was found in her thin coat and worn shoes . . . under a boarded sidewalk. It was a stone's throw from the police station and the hall.

Twenty

"You meet such interesting people."

No matter what your profession, you're bound to have tired old clichés thrown at you. Is there a doctor in the house? Here come de judge. Written any good books lately? The postman always knocks twice. Ours in the newspaper business — not "game", please, f'r Godsake — is the "interesting people" syndrome. (Another, in my case, especially from well-to-do socialites: "I've always thought I'd enjoy writing those little pieces you do, if I had time. My teachers used to say . . . .")

You do net some rare birds, whose feathers may be preened to less effect than they imagine. One who comes handily to mind is Nancy Reagan, the erstwhile film actress who became the second wife of Ronald Reagan, stage and film leading man of the '40s and '50s. Reagan was, of course, later elected governor of California and held the job for several years. As I write, he has vigorous presidential ambitions. By the way, if you ever encounter the Reagans, it's pronounced Raygan, not Reegan, as I was quickly corrected to note.

We met in 1967. Reagan, who once played a not insignificant off-stage role in helping Senator Joseph McCarthy bring a new and sinister dimension to the designation "right wing" in politics, had just won office as a Republican in the U.S.A.'s most populous state. The performer turned politician was still a novelty. I arrived at the lovely old capitol building in its flowered and leafy park setting just in time for a press conference and was most impressed with the new governor's skill in that selective bearpit. I had watched President Dwight Eisenhower at a White House conference, bumbling his way along, constantly calling on nearby aides for figures, facts, etc., or frequently having them come forward hastily with whispered corrections. Reagan was efficient, to the point, very articulate, and amazingly well-informed, down to minute statistic and detail. He was concise, answered questions without prior submission from the press corps, and by-passed the cosy use of first names I've found employed so often for favourites. When I interviewed him later, he left no doubt about his hawk-like intentions in Viet Nam. ("I want them to go to bed every night wondering if we will use nuclear weapons.")

Next day — the governor's mansion for a scheduled talk with Mrs. Reagan. My reception was something of a surprise, for a press secretary had said to me cheerfully on the telephone, "Sure. Nancy will be free that day."

Mrs. Reagan greeted me in a big sprawling reception area, and we moved towards the drawing-room. I wanted to take my coat off, get my notebook out, and perhaps sit down. There was no such suggestion. We both stood.

The small, slight woman seemed somewhat on the defensive, and so I began by commenting on the many pieces of old furniture I could see around the room. "Of course, they're not real antiques," she said quickly. "They were here when we came." Her tone suggested I

171

might have had the perspicacity to avoid this *faux pas* in the realm of good taste.

I asked if I might remove my coat and sit down. She settled gingerly in a nearby chair and seemed to have nothing further to say.

"It's a fine old residence," I noted.

Mrs. Reagan waved a hand around disparagingly. "It's also a firetrap. Besides, it's not a good neighbourhood for the children." What's-that-again? I thought. If a gubernatorial mansion doesn't set the tone of the area, what does? "We're moving as soon as we can find a place in the right kind of residential district."

Whatever path I took, the conversation seemed off-key. She lifted an eyebrow when I didn't recognize the names of the private schools her children attended and had to ask the spelling. When I wondered if she made a favourite dish for her husband, she cut me down quickly with, "I don't cook and I rarely go into the kitchen." But she had immediately redone her husband's new office in antiques and dark-stained panelling. She was an ardent Junior Leaguer.

I cannot remember another occasion on which I was able to gain so little rapport with a so-called willing subject. I think I began to find out why when she pointed out very firmly that she'd really gone to Hollywood in the first place out of boredom with the debutante scene in Chicago, where her stepfather was an eminent neurosurgeon. Her mother had been a singer, she noted.

I later mentioned to one of the best-known stars of the American theatre that I felt Mrs. R. had been rather rude. "Why should she be rude to you?" she wondered. "She was rude to me, but I think that was because I spoke of her mother as having been in the chorus."

No, Mrs. Reagan went on, as Nancy Davis she had not fallen in love with a movie actor when she met and married her husband. She wanted to make that very clear. "I was a young actress and apparently there was another, or were others, of the name Nancy Davis in Hollywood. I was getting mail from Communist-front organizations. I told Mervyn LeRoy (the director) of my concern. 'You should see Ronald Reagan,' he said. And then, 'You two would get along very well.' "

It was the early 1950s. Senator McCarthy was masterminding a witch hunt that made Salem's seem like a Sunday school corn roast. Hysteria in the House of Representatives Un-American Activities Committee sent accusations spewing out in all directions of "communists" rotting the fabric of every aspect of the American way of life.

Hollywood was especially hard hit by the McCarthy tarbrush. Reagan was president of the 8000-strong Screen Actors Guild and, as Mrs. Reagan told me, grappling with what he saw as the scourge of communism in the industry.

"He was a strong man. That's what attracted me, and our joint interest in stamping it out."

The invidious net spread to tangle, sometimes strangle, the careers of so many of the most talented and most popular actors, producers, directors, and writers in the film capital with "leftist tendencies". In an article for *The Chicago Tribune* Press Service of July 29, 1951, Seymour Korman described Ronald Reagan as one of "the men who have most vigorously fought the Red Menace (in Hollywood)".

"Penetrate the veneer and mumbo-jumbo conversation of a Hollywood Communist, particularly of the 'intellectual' type," he quotes Reagan as saying, "and you'll frequently discover a person bothered by some neurosis. Those people might otherwise have a phony religion to alleviate their frustrations."

These were the people bent on the destruction of the American dream? Lucille Ball, Larry Parks, Sterling Hayden, Frederic March, Edward G. Robinson, José Ferrer, John Garfield, Judy Holliday? Saddest of all, perhaps, were many of the terrified "confessions" and ratting on others under suspicion. "We must encourage those who recant, as the police encouage stool pigeons," said author Rupert Hughes, one of the "big three" mentioned glowingly in Seymour Korman's *Chicago Tribune* story.

So I think I began to understand why Mrs. Reagan and I didn't seem to be able to achieve much rapport. Of course, it is claimed most Canadians tend to be Democrats at heart, especially since the days of Presidents Franklin Roosevelt and John Kennedy. So I must, in my own defence, say that I found Peggy Goldwater, wife of the Republican Senator who won the presidential nomination for his party in 1964, to be one of the most charming and "comfortable" of women.

Goldwater had just won the nomination, and I followed a routine similar to that with the Reagans, sitting in first at a press conference with the candidate. I found him an interesting and vital man, charming, volatile, and with occasional show of quick temper. He's a skilled pilot and an avid ham radio fan; one whole corner of the Arizona red ledge stone house, contoured into the hilltop, is given over to his highly sophisticated equipment.

Like Nancy Reagan, Peggy Goldwater had come from a wealthy family, but she was a woman with amusement and tranquillity in her deep blue eyes and was obviously the centre of an ebullient and affectionate clan. The day I visited, a cheery house guest, widow of the cowboy star Harry Carey, was broiling hamburgers and deftly sandwiching them between buns for the then young sons. A terrier puppy teased a massive old bulldog by the open kitchen fireside. Amid all the activity, Mrs. Goldwater serenely made iced tea.

"I married a young businessman running the department store the family owned," she said with a wry little smile, "and when Barry went into politics after coming back from World War II, I knew whatever he wanted was right with me." But her political activity was strictly off-stage. Her great interests were the Red Cross, a hospital board, the YWCA, and a planned parenthood organization, which she had helped organize and, at the time of my visit, headed as president.

The Goldwaters have been great campers in the senator's beloved mountains and valleys of Arizona, and she said, with an affectionate grin, "I cook Barry's favourite steaks and chocolate puddings and listen when he wants to think out something — and all our married life I've picked up the things he's strewn about."

My favourite Republican wife, Mrs. Goldwater. I came away as warmed as I had been chilled in Sacramento.

Mrs. Lyndon Johnson, when I interviewed her, was of a distinctly different breed from either of these. Ladybird, which has to be the most incredible nickname for any American president's wife, was shrewd, affable, but never friendly to the point of gush, as Mrs. Nixon sometimes seemed to be.

I always felt a little sorry for Pat Nixon; she seemed so eager to be liked. In my experience when she was at the White House or I was in a press party involved with the Nixons in other cities, there was more than the natural graciousness of a first lady. It was almost pathetic at times. Now, of course, in hindsight, there could have been the desire to over-compensate for her husband's backstage behaviour and crudeness of language.

But Ladybird knew exactly where she was going and what she was doing. Her experience as a radio-station owner and in other business ventures had given her an executive approach to her job as wife of the president of the United States. She was completely organized, down to the last touch of lipstick and faultless hairdo. I suspect she is one of those rare women who carry uncluttered and well-ordered handbags.

Ladybird and her press secretary Liz Carpenter worked together with perfect understanding and communication. More than once, following Ladybird with a press group, I've been pulled aside by Liz with the sharp command: "Get out of the way! The television cameras are on the president's wife!'' Like an army sergeant-major, Liz vetted and directed those of us allowed in to White House events. On one such occasion I found myself excluded from among the chosen few to be present when Ladybird would receive a group of women achievers (known around the country as Ladybird's do-gooders) in the voluntary service line. Always working on the premise that you push forward until they stop you, I waited in an anteroom outside the reception area, hoping I might somehow gain entrance, perhaps unobserved. (A not very likely prospect — Liz already knew me well.)

Along came Carol Channing, the comedienne and actress and an old friend, with husband Charles Lowe. Charles noted me sitting dejectedly in a corner and came over heartily and we all kissed and hugged (me with more fervour and visibility than I customarily display).

Carol was a favourite of the Johnsons and had come to entertain and charm the visiting firewomen. We walked together into the inner sanctum, arms linked, and I had more success with both the presidential family and Liz after that.

But none of the American political hierarchy could fill the widely travelled shoes of one of the great human beings of my generation. It required no Democratic leaning to find Eleanor Roosevelt one of the truly great women of my experience.

I had met the widow of the president of the United States in an elevator aboard ship. Time was when I went out with the pilot and press party in New York, sometimes, to interview VIPs aboard incoming vessels. That day, Mrs. Roosevelt was returning from Geneva, where she had been at a meeting of the United Nations. (She headed the Human Rights Committee for some time.) Also on board was an anthropologist, whose name I do not now recall, claiming to have found the elusive missing link between man and ape. Because Eleanor Roosevelt's story would not be wildly newsworthy and since the two press interviews had been scheduled simultaneously in different lounges, I was one of the handful who opted for the lady. She left quietly alone, and I followed into an elevator.

There were just two of us. Very quickly I expressed my long-held desire to have an interview with her in depth on her home ground. Almost to my surprise, she asked for my card. (It still is considered a little fancy for reporters to request business cards from their newspapers. I just got tired of scribbling identity and credentials on a scrap of copy paper and made a pitch. The *Star* has always obliged.) "You will hear from me," she said, and we parted.

I did, indeed, hear from her before long. It was mid-summer of 1948, and in her neat, small backhand writing came directions for an informal and leisurely appointment. To my delight, she was receiving me at her country cottage Val-Kill (Dutch for "Brook in the Fields") in the hills high above Hyde Park. I took a creaky local train from Albany, New York, to the little Hyde Park Station. Herman, a grizzled elderly man who was the mail station messenger, was at the station in his 1937 Plymouth coach, loading groceries and mail from the train.

He'd known the Roosevelts for forty years. "Franklin was as clever as they come," he said in his nasal drawl. "Knew how to referee a baseball game with the best, out at the high school, before he took sick. And I wish you could of heard the speech he made when we opened the town post office."

We climbed a country road and came to a stone cottage with a neat white sign reading: "Careful. Children and Horses."

"I wouldn't stay long," Herman offered. "She's pretty busy right now."

I nodded quickly. "I know — the autobiography, her newspaper column, work with the United Nations . . . ."

"Raspberries," he interrupted drily. "It's raspberry season and she's got quite a pile of bushes up here. And the grandchildren — never less'n eight or ten a week up here and at Elliott's place along the road.''

True. I was greeted by an apologetic secretary just as one of the grandchildren arrived by bicycle and started scrounging for cookies in the kitchen.

I sat in the comfortable living-room. It was book-scattered, with chintz-covered chairs and chesterfield (neatly mended in a couple of places) and lead-paned windows with green leaves etched against them from the sheltering trees outside. There were well-thumbed children's books and flowers. Only certain kinds of women, I thought, go into the fields and gather great armfuls of black-eyed Susans; kneel to pick a hundred pansies and float them in a soup tureen; fill a green pitcher with orange and yellow nasturtiums.

She came in with the dogs — a country grandmother in a pink seersucker dress, her wavy hair brushed back, her clear skin sunned and freckled. Her country basket was well filled with berries, and, as we sipped coffee and munched cookies, she picked up some knitting and made me at ease.

In the next hours (I ignored Herman's advice), we ranged over a great deal of her life and thoughts, and I remember some of the things she said, in her careful phrasing, as though it were yesterday. She believed in self-disicipline — she was glad she had learned it as a girl — and she liked to make her own bed, do physical work.

She spoke of growing old. ''To grow old is to grow patient,'' she said, ''for in slowing you down physically, nature also makes you aware that a great many things you hoped for in the world won't happen tomorrow or the next day.''

We talked of the late president, his triumphs and defeats. ''Franklin's greatest defeats came in his later years when he saw the vision of things that might be and were not. These were the deep and spiritual failures that affected us both very strongly.''

Of her children: "I was with them a great deal and nursed them through all their childhood illnesses; I wish now, though, I could have taught them more wisdom, saved them more heartaches and mistakes."

She felt her husband's greatest contribution to his own country, perhaps the world, had been his ability through his voice and way of speaking to give a sense of security at a time when it was most needed to help people overcome their fears.

I've thought of her so many times since, especially when I have been at the United Nations in New York, for here, she thought, lay the hope, if we had hope, for the future of mankind. "The basic fact of being a human being must carry with it, in itself, the right to respect. That is what the U.N. must be all about." So I always stop into the little non-denominational chapel at the U.N. and think of that.

Twenty-One

Many of today's free-wheeling journalists could beat me hands down on knowledge or experience of the world scene — like the top pros of my own newspaper: Jack Cahill, Mark Gayn, Marilyn Dunlop, Frank Jones, Gerald Utting, Jack Brehl, and George Bain, to name a few. The *Star* is a great on-the-trouble-spot staffer, so much so that I'd like to have made publication of this book conditional on a dust-jacket sticker marked: "**WARNING.** Contents could cause digestive distress to foreign correspondents over 21."

But I'll match my by-line with any claimants when it comes to all-out coverage of this country Canada, from whose roots I spring and with whose people I have long shared national wonders and blunders, prairie bread and Ottawa circuses, and the Canuck way of life from ocean to ocean to ocean (the status one's the Arctic). I've criss-crossed the skies uncountable times; travelled by rail, bus, car, boat, horse, tractor, sled, bicycle, jeep, trailer, and many a mile on foot, in every direction from that thin line of major population shadowed by the United States. I can't think of a city I haven't been in, and I live in the heart of the biggest English-speaking one, Toronto, at the corner of Bay and Bloor Streets, the heart-beat of the metropolis. I love the crowds and roaring rhythms of downtown as much as the lone and quiet places far away, always somewhere in the bottom of my mind.

Where to start? I see life largely in terms of people against their situations and backgrounds, and so I think of the captain of a little fishing vessel in Conception Bay, Newfoundland, on an occasion when the huge silver-blue tuna were running. My then managing editor at the *Star,* Harry Hindemarsh, walked into the city room one day with the news of a great inshore surge of finny mammoths. It meant that, probably for the first time, an average middle-income neophyte could indulge in what had been a sport of millionaires. He looked around for the most unlikely deep-sea fisherman on staff.

"Fish? No, Harry. I've never even caught a minnow." But a few hours later a big "Gone Fishin' " sign had been hung on my typewriter; I was outfitted with slicker and sou'wester and dispatched to the Canadian Far East.

Once strapped into the anchored chair astern the boat and given instruction by a disbelieving crew, I was terrified — even more so when there came a tug on the line like an elephant on demolition fatigue. The captain, a rugged and weathered man, saw my dilemma and came to the rescue, taking over the rod while others began getting out clubs with which to finish off the shimmering creature, now surfacing like a miniature submarine.

"Look lively! There'll be a lot of blood," shouted someone. I prayed our catch would get away. I was aware the fish was not required for food. So easy had been the kill for so many that townsfolk were coming down to the wharf with pails and tubs and filling them. These are not the tuna we ordinarily receive tinned, but a much saltier, stronger-tasting variety. No, this was purely a sporting event.

"He's off the hook!" yelled the skipper to the dismayed assemblage and my relief. I suspect he knew how to lose as well as bring in a big one. He pretended sympathy, in a face-saving way, then began to talk of the island and the island people; the rocks and birds and flowers and forest streams, and the long, harsh winters. He was a plain-spoken man, not given to superlatives (few Canadians are, in the outreaches), but his love for this remote, sea-circled place came through sure and strong.

And I think of the men of the forests I have met, of their rapport with the wilderness of woods, and of the lumber camps. I flew into a camp in the interior of northern Ontario once with the late Frank McDougal, when he was Deputy Minister of Lands and Forests for the province. I remember the tenderness with which this veteran bush pilot and high-ranking civil servant from Toronto touched tiny shoots planted in reforestation projects, to replace the mighty giants being felled, and his story of the wonder of how trees grow.

I've picked apples with growers in the rich Okanagan Valley of British Columbia, aware of the bounty of their orchards; and climbed high mountain trails with game wardens and fire rangers, who know and respect the animals, and the trust we hold in keeping this country strong and life-sustaining for those yet to come. I've ridden with the engineer and fireman of a huge diesel engine through a vast and far-reaching wilderness of wooded northland, as they pointed out and identified every bird and animal trail we passed en route and talked of the deep and hidden recesses far beyond the railways and the roads, where they and their families go by boat.

And there's Prince Edward Island and the Maritimes, where, in October, frost-touched leaves blazed for miles like an unearthly fire. "The scarlet of the maples can shake me like a cry, of bugles going by. And my lonely spirit thrills, to

Lotta tuna-fishing in Conception Bay, Newfoundland, in August 1961.

Lotta ready to set sail on the *Norweta* in 1971.

see the frosty asters like a smoke upon the hills," wrote Canadian poet Bliss Carmen. Robert Service, poet of the Canadian North, tells of the aurora borealis, weaving and lacing the sky with banners of greens and blues and purples, and I have lain in wonder in the fields to watch. No, you can't know this country in your heart's blood, without being caught up in its innards — its raw, compelling pull to the basic relationship of man and environment.

But coastal surfbeat, glacial timelessness, the woven shade of forest, and the sweep of great lake or prairie cannot compare with the primeval and elementary force of the Arctic. So I think of Canadians I've met there, like Captain Don Tetrault, one-time ocean-roving, salvage ship captain, who went to the Northwest Territories on a routine job and stayed to become part of it. To me he symbolizes the new younger breed of knowledgeable, concerned Canadians, aware of how carefully the country must be opened up and what disaster there can be if we do not follow the immutable laws of nature.

Working out of the small town of Hay River on the Alberta-Territories border, Tetrault visualized a small passenger boat to carry travellers the 1500 miles down the great MacKenzie River to the ocean. But the native Montrealer got short shrift from financiers in eastern Canada to whom he went for backing. The summer season would be too brief. Flying was the accepted and established mode of transportation in this country. Blackflies and mosquitoes would deter tourists. (They haven't Queen Elizabeth and Prince Philip, Prince Charles and Princess Anne, although it is strange to see the familiar royal visages smeared with protective oily lotion.)

Don Tetrault is a man of some steel, and so he got together a group of Hay River citizens, and they sat around somebody's dining-room table and formed a company with personal pledges. The ship was designed specifically for these often treacherous waters, which can spread from narrow, high-cliffed passages to widths of a mile, with white water rapids or rocky shoals for the unwary. Tetrault and other seasoned rivermen know every mood and contour and current of the river.

I took the journey in the first season of operation, in the early 1970s, and it was quite the most memorable of my travels anywhere, at home or abroad.

Before he launched the *Norweta* (short for Northwest Territories, named through a contest for schoolchildren in the area), Don prepared the people we would meet as carefully as he did his chart — and his passengers. There were just a dozen of us (the boat has been somewhat enlarged since), and the skipper spent days visiting every trading post, Indian and Eskimo settlement, R.C.M.P. station, Hudson's Bay operation, fishermen's village, environmental control centre, oil consortium, and fur and Eskimo and Indian art agency to explain our interest. We were seeking to learn more of this great country and its people, not to gape at the natives or complain about the sometimes primitive conditions.

Although we had come in the spirit of the venture, well versed in the history and current development of the territory, Don had an extensive library aboard for our further enlightenment. Looking after us in the ship and ashore were highly competent young Indian and Eskimo people. This book isn't about the Canadian Far North, the beauty of its short-flowering summer, the changes as civilization comes in on oil-drilling rig and scow and truck. Or of the efforts of the government and others concerned to keep the environment and the native people free from harm or debasement. But I remember following a little flock of beautiful Eskimo boys and girls in Tuktoyaktuk as they took us shyly but courteously to see their pingo, the huge, always-frozen cave in which the men of the community put their hunting kill for each family to share according to need. (They only kill what they must have for food.) And what a weird sort of museum it was, for the animals are left intact in fur and skin until butchered.

So, as they say in the travelogues, on to other times and places. One amusing thing: I brought back a large piece of curiously marked rock and took it to the Royal Ontario Museum for identification. Back came a neatly typed piece of paper, which noted that while this stone was half a million years old, "it is not a very well preserved specimen".

Canadians? We have as many facets as our country. I do not know of anywhere in the world, in my experience, where one can find as culturally seasoned, charming, and elegant men and women as in the old and settled parts of French Canada. Through the ancient Laurentian Mountains, in clubs and hotel lounges and old residences of Montreal and Quebec City, there is a special breed of Canadian, sophisticated and urbane. Prime Minister Pierre Elliott Trudeau is one of many of his ilk. They are city people or country people of cosmopolitan background. I've been to a sugaring-off party where the women's snowsuits all came from Paris and the men wore hand-crafted shirts and jackets. The best-dressed Canadians, and often, I think, those with the greatest *joie de vivre,* live and move in this, *la belle province.*

In contrast to these so-French people are the Victorian old guard of Vancouver Island. In fact, we are a country of contrasts. The big metropolis of Toronto has become, in many ways, representative of the international mix of Canada, its influx of newcomers from all over the world giving what was once a staid old WASP town a United Nations flavour. Can we pull it all together? My faith lies in the profound Canadianism somewhere deep in what we call our national mosaic (as opposed to melting pot). I think of leaders fiercely fighting for what they consider the rights of their own provinces — often, in pre-oil shortage days, underprivileged provinces.

So what is a Canadian? How did we get to be our peculiar and recognizable breed of North American? I think I found out very early in life.

When American relatives gathered at my grandparents' home in Seattle, Washington, usually once a year, affectionately overspilling the middle-sized house, I always was presented as, "And this is our little Canadian grandchild," or, "This is our niece (cousin, whatever) from Canada."

All but my mother had mated within the eagle's nest, spreading from California to Alaska. I sensed that however warmly I was accepted into this close-knit blood community, I was considered somewhat different, that I was designated as from the most distant as well as the most alien port of family call. I went well armed with "shinplasters", little 25-cent paper bills which at one time were a curious output of the Canadian treasury, and found these viable items of trade with the Americans, who regarded them rather like wampum beads. I was teased, without malice, over my pronunciations of "hoose" and "moose" and my "zed" instead of "zee" at alphabet's end.

They also asked numerous puzzling questions about the king and queen and how we felt about them. I had no feeling. They were just there on our schoolroom walls; I took it for granted, like singing *God Save the King*, although I never was convinced we could exert much influence, being so far from Buckingham Palace and all. It was all just part of how we were, like the legislative buildings and the Saskatchewan River at the end of our street in Edmonton.

I considered my American visits deliciously abandoned, something of a cross between visiting Sodom and Gomorrah and the Disneyland of today. Movies on Sunday, when I had not been allowed even to cut out pictures at home. Happy jaunts on open-sided streetcars to the roller-coaster downtown section and the ship-cluttered waterfront. Eating in restaurants and cafeterias — at home this was considered a sybaritic if not, indeed, dissipated practice, like taking taxis.

Wandering around huge department stores. Going to afternoon matinées in vaudeville houses, where little boxes of candies fastened to the backs of seats were available for a dime or quarter in a slot.

Then, my grandfather's big shiny barber shop, with all the chairs and pungent smells and lather, and razors being stropped by the jolly young men he employed; the American silver dollars and creamy chocolate eclairs, and laughter running through my grandparents' house in this free and easy and often quite zany community of kinfolk.

So I began to think very early about what a Canadian was and why, and how we differed from our American compatriots across the border. The contrast was marked in my Canadian grandparents' home in Stratford, Ontario, where rules and protocol, even for a young child, made life seem very relaxed in Edmonton, let alone Seattle. No one ever questioned the portrait of Queen Victoria severely dominating the front parlour. Or the twice-a-day church on Sunday, the morning service followed by the solemn trek to the town graveyard to tend the plots of those in the family connection who had passed on, of which there were many. Or the constant visits back and forth with relatives who all seemed very, very old, bearded or ankle-skirted, hard of hearing, and straight-laced.

Yet somehow, with the clarity children have before they learn to double-think, I knew this was my heritage, my strong strain. This Irish Canadian grandfather, who had come over on a sailing ship as a young man, cleared land for the farm, helped build the church with other neighbours, planted trees as well as grain. Once he walked, with a friend, nine miles to get two wooden cradles available to first comers. He was in the process of fathering nine sturdy children. The other fellow, family lore had it, found the heavy piece of furniture too much of a burden, and my grandfather ended up carrying both back.

And my grandmother, weighing no more than 90 to 100 pounds, walking three miles to town to sell the eggs and home again, when the men couldn't spare the horses. Sure, my American grandfather had made a mile-long swim across the Mississippi River as a boy; he used to recount it with pride. But he never told me *why*.

And all these years, as I have gone to various parts of the world and tried to understand and be one with other members of our family of man, I never have been in doubt as to which branch I belong. I began, as I grew older, to try to analyze as honestly and accurately as I could, what it was to *feel* Canadian. And I found, as I became a reporter and travelled and interviewed my countrymen of high and low estate in almost every nook and cranny of this half-continent, that most of us had in some way been shaped by the land or the waters thereof.

We were as marked by the early loneliness and harshness of our legacy as by the varied bloodstreams in our veins. Whether we are late or newcome, something of that clings — a stubborn authority exerted by the vast, sprawling terrain itself, because wherever we live in the awesome spread of city-seashore-mountain-forest-prairie-tundra, we are never far from its natural strength and power to sustain or defeat us.

It has shaped our culture to such an extent that only now, more than a century past Confederation and nationhood, are we getting around to plumbing the relationship of human beings to one another, apart from environment, and to their inner selves.

We are bound, or released, by the geographic and demographic facts of a few million people largely scattered (other than the few big-city enclaves, widely spaced) across 3000 miles, along a narrow corridor bordering the United States, with a population ten times ours. So another of our character-forming agents, as Canadians, is the fact that we have no heartland. This came home to me strongly when the editor of a U.S. magazine for whom I had done some pieces sent me a clipping of an article on the American heartland. He asked for a comparable story from Canada. I tried three times, failing miserably, and finally wrote: "There just isn't any, in a physical sense. We're indigenous to our various widely different home places. When our Canadian heartland develops — and it is shaping and materializing — it will be a cultural, emotional, and in-the-bone thing.

"We will grow into our Canadian heartland, through our writers and artists and singers and broadcasters; and through our coming to share understanding of all the land that holds us in fee."

Today we are the late twentieth-century explorers of our own psyche and history, and especially of the country itself.

As a reporter I've covered the Calgary Stampede, Edmonton's Klondike Days, Highland Games in the Maritimes, and that peculiarly national football fiesta, the Grey Cup, in big-city stadiums; hundreds of homecoming weeks, old home gatherings, centennials, and other chest-expanding regional events.

You know what I always find? Scratch the staunchest local from any part you like, and you'll find a bone-Canadian underneath.

Twenty-Two

American humorist-poet Ogden Nash once wrote some verses about the very rich, in which he noted:

> The only incurable troubles of the rich are the troubles that money can't cure,
> Which is a kind of trouble that is even more troublesome if you are poor.
> Certainly there are lots of things in life that money won't buy, but it's very funny —
> Have you ever tried to buy them without money?

And who was it who said — "I've been poor and I've been rich. Rich is better." A good many people, like Frank Sinatra, have expressed something of that philosophy — those who, like old Blue Eyes, have hacked it from burger-on-a-bun to beef Wellington, traded beer for bubbly, and left the cross-country bus far behind in a luxurious private jet.

Since the days of the pharaohs people have had a lively curiosity about the ways of life of those who inherit or accumulate fortunes. How do they use the energy they don't need in the struggle to pay bills, budget family purchases, hold a steady job, or take chances on new ventures? What do they shop for, who never have to face the bank manager or a finance company?

I suppose one of the privileges of the working press is access to so many of the rich and powerful. My husband, a capable architect, used to shake his head in mystification when he first became accessory to some of my labours. Just why, he pondered, did this particular trade, among a myriad serving the public, rate ringside seats and privileged entrée almost anywhere? "Because," I said, "we put their names in the paper."

And Dick made one of his shrewd comments on this particular presumption: "So okay, lady newshound. But don't ever forget it isn't your baby-blue eyes they fall for. It's your baby-blue print."

Like other reporters, I am sure, I've made some close and lasting friends through the job. But overall, I've never confused the power of the press with personal relationships. Nothing plugs out so fast as a disconnected by-line. One of the finest news staffers I knew noted this a short time after she resigned from a big metropolitan daily. "You wouldn't believe how soon your name is erased from all the party lists and how quickly you become 'what's-her-name'. Most of those charmers who wanted your 'advice' or the pleasure of your company for lunch at expensive restaurants or as guests at their soirées suffer galloping amnesia."

Be that as it may, you do join the first-class passengers on their journey through life for whatever part of the trip your schedule may be slated. Your footprints usually are those next on the red carpet for everything from royal personages and heads of state to superstars of sport, science, entertainment, and the arts.

It has amusing aspects. On occasion I've watched members of the Establishment, especially the wives, practically go to the bathroom in euphoria over bowing or curtsying to royalty, lining up to shake a super-politico's hand, or basking momentarily in the radiance of a current star. Yet I've been one of a press group chatting and lifting a glass with them informally an hour before. Another day, another year, another reporter will be in my place, wearing the magic pass on a jacket lapel. But it's lovely while it lasts, and the imprint is indelible.

How do the rich, the powerful, and the creatively favoured children of the gods live? When Charles Templeton was managing editor of *The Toronto Star,* he called me to his office one day. "Average readers brush the very wealthy only when they see them sabled, jewelled, and dinner-jacketed at theatre and gallery openings or pictured at weddings, charity affairs, and other such events. How do they live at home?"

I agreed it was a subject of natural curiosity.

"Then pick ten of the most affluent families in the public eye and find out."

I did, and although I won't go into the series of stories and pictures that resulted in the *Star,* there were certain common denominators I found, both in that project and through many other opportunities. There is a kind of understated mellow ambience, especially among those long established in the affluent tradition — a climatic well-being that comes from more than flawless airconditioning, indoor swimming pools, or a plenitude of service to hold the dust down. Wealth can provide an efficacious spray-can to keep under control all the gnatty little aggravations suffered by so many of the rest of us. Living tends to be personalized — one has one's own special perfumier, designer, decorator, stationer, gentleman's tailor and haberdasher. When you are accustomed to wealth, you dress properly for every time and place. That can mean worn comfort at moments of lazy relaxation. I remember once at Hyannisport, Massachusetts, when I was doing some stories on the Kennedy family just after John Kennedy's election to the U.S. presidency. The most sensibly and simply dressed children I saw were those of the Kennedy clan. I watched a clutch of them one day following an old man in a floppy fisherman's hat, faded blue shirt, and worn white shorts. He was Joseph P. Kennedy, the multimillionaire paterfamilias. But you should have seen the boat they boarded, berthed at the private Kennedy dock.

Queen Elizabeth is pictured in simple peasant-type headscarves, worn tweeds, and sturdy boots when she's around her racing stables. But brother, get a load of those horses.

For social or state affairs, the rich and powerful dress with a sense of occasion. They gleam and glitter. You ought to catch Rose Kennedy in her real milieu at Palm Beach. She's magnificently groomed. To me, Pat Nixon never quite achieved the air of built-in elegance the Kennedys have. Whatever she wore, it still seemed like a neat business-girl party dress taken from the rack.

Those of long-established place in the social ladder, like Rose Kennedy, have a certain quiet authority about them. Once when I interviewed her, she asserted it without apparent effort. We were on a television program for the Canadian Broadcasting Corporation. The director started talking of preparations for a customary rehearsal. (I had already interviewed Mrs. Kennedy for my newspaper.) She gently but firmly demurred, having glanced through my suggested questions.

"I think we know what we are going to say," she said. And *she* certainly knew.

In my observation, the greatest boon of affluence is the luxury of *lebensraum* — spaced-out living and privacy. (If I were run-of-mill Chinese or Russian, as I am Canadian, I would find the crowding of families into small quarters the most difficult of my sacrifices for ideological fulfilment.)

193

Then, too, the rich can find, unless they're really poisonous (and a few are), their choice of company from among the world's most talented and stimulating people.

"Why don't you spend more time with the kind of people you came from?" I once asked a very prosperous Canadian who had been a penniless boy.

He answered without a tinge of embarrassment, "Because I've worked so hard to get away from us. We were very dull."

A majority of the very rich take first-class passage on any venture as divine right. Exception: Lord Thomson of Fleet, the multimillionaire Canadian-turned-British-peer and press tycoon. Now in his eighties Roy Thomson may have dispensed with his long custom of flying economy. But it was a first-class place in Westminster Abbey he was kind enough to pass on to me when he found himself unable to attend the coronation of Queen Elizabeth II.

"First-class" means private clubs where your favourite drink and cigar, and how you like your steak done, are tenets of the staff; and you never wait in line for dinner, golf, or a place at the bridge table or the tennis court. It means time and climate for the niceties of communication, the graciousness people can afford when they don't have to fight for a place in the sun or out of the rain. "The Queen (or the wife of the governor-general or the Empress of Iran) is so gracious," people say. One is tempted to wonder if it isn't fairly easy, with no parking, baby-sitting, or bargain-sale maulings to cope with.

All this non-trespass territory is well defended and surrounded by an invisible but highly charged fence. The way in? Well, first you have to have the scratch. Then, as I've told a few come-lately affluents imprudent enough to seek advice of a reporter with grocery store credentials, there are race horses, big boats, charities, cultural groupie-hood, and the right kind of sports. The men serve on boards; women join committees. Still, it doesn't always work. I know of very rich men seeking sponsorship and acceptance in elite clubs without success.

It's funny about money. Everybody wants it, but if you have it, you don't talk about it. I remember how shocked one wealthy host was when Sir Tyrone Guthrie, the great Irish director and producer, asked a direct question over a cocktail.

"Are you very rich?" he wanted to know, as casually as he might have enquired about the pedigreed livestock on the estate. I refrained from asking the Establishment man his response.

For some reason, for many years the Canadian who seemed most to epitomize top-bracket wealth in my country was industrialist Edward Plunkett Taylor. There are a number of low-profile multis with as much or more moolah simmering away on the back burners. But Taylor was highly visible, as business tycoon, race-horse man, and philanthropist who made many gifts to his city and country.

Until he established his main residence in Nassau, the name of the big, well-groomed man was a by-word in conversations every day. A wife asking for dress money, an office worker seeking more pay, a child coaxing pennies for corner-store goodies, would be asked, "Who do you think I am? E. P. Taylor?" It was the Canadian version of the Rockefeller syndrome.

Once in my column in *The Toronto Star* I quoted from an American newspaper, which reported that green fees on the golf course in Lyford Cay, Mr. Taylor's residential development in the Bahamas, were $100 a day. Posthaste I had a call from the gentleman to say that this was highly overstated. We chatted about the 4000-acre estate he had designed as an exclusive colony, and he suggested I drop over and look for myself. (You see the power of even an incorrect item in the press?)

I did, when next in those parts, and it was a fascinating visit. No one could have been a better or more thoughtful host to my husband and me and two friends.

Mr. Taylor met us at the always-guarded entrance. "This is as far as you could come without me," he said cheerfully. We had a leisurely tour of the whole area, and my husband, being an architect, was intrigued with how whole hills and valleys had been man-made to enhance the contours. The houses, built often to client specification by the Taylor interests, were of fine design and standard. Arthur Hailey, the best-selling author *(The Moneychangers, Hotel, Airport,* etc.), and his wife Sheila live there. I had known them in their days as fellow-staffers at MacLean-Hunter.

Taylor pointed out the private telephone, police, and fire services, the fine country club, churches, the aforementioned golf course, then took us to his own house to have pre-lunch martinis with Mrs. Taylor.

The residence is set on a long neck of land, so situated that the aquamarine sea and beige-powder sand can be seen from windows and patios on both sides. This was at a time when President John Kennedy and his official party had just been guests of the Taylors, when the American came for a conference with then Prime Ministers Harold MacMillan of Britain and John Diefenbaker of Canada.

The Taylors vacated for President Kennedy's stay. Mrs. Taylor satisfied my natural curiosity as to where the president had slept by showing me her own suite, and I expressed surprise that he didn't use the more masculine one across the hall, that of Mr. Taylor. It had something to do with greater security, assessed by an advance party checking on the accommodation. Security men stayed in the master suite.

So big, handsome John Kennedy slept in a dainty single bed under a pale pink silken canopy and used a pink boudoir and lavender and moss green bathroom. The Taylors had gone to some lengths to obtain a rocking chair that seemed similar to the president's much-favoured one, but he brought his own. This gave credence in my mind to the rumours, later confirmed, of Kennedy's serious back problems. Further comment on this would seem to have been the meticulous care with which the advance guard tested the small residence-type elevator between main and second floor, riding up and down several times. It was pointed out that wide, gently-spaced few steps were close by, but no — Kennedy would be using the elevator.

So there you have one small private world of built-in space, beauty, and luxury. That's rich, kids.

Finally, I have a favourite multimillionaire. It is that grand old man whose intellectual and moral backbone has been too tough for any amount of attempted wreckage over his 90-some years, Cyrus Eaton.

I have no reason to change in any way the assessment I made of the Canadian-born industrialist and intellectual in the mid-1960s when I spend a weekend at his lovely old farm home in Deep Cove, Nova Scotia. Or after attending sessions of the international Thinkers' Conference, which he sponsored in his birthplace, Pugwash, Nova Scotia.

I reported then: "History will write him big. He's one of the biggest backstage technicians in this sombre, holocaust-triggered drama of the 20th century.

"If there is to be a 21st, Cleveland magnate Cyrus Eaton could even be monumentalized as a soft-spoken intellectual who at times single-handedly kept the East-West Global sound track from going dead. He might be rated as a member of a tiny guild which forestalled the black-out of the human race."

Any newspaper file on this continent will tell you the story of Cyrus Eaton's clear-eyed struggles against unbelievable censure and, indeed, strong pressures in the United States to put him down in his top-echelon contacts with the U.S.S.R. and China. But it is the informal Cyrus Eaton I remember, a man close to the land and the people.

Life in Deep Cove is simple, close to nature, and utterly relaxing — except that I found it difficult to keep pace with this wiry climber, sailor, and fast walker. There were no other guests that weekend, and so it meant long hours of rich talk around the open fireplace with Eaton and his lovely wife Anne. Conversation ranged easily from his close knowledge of and, indeed, friendship with the leaders of the U.S.S.R., through country cattle talk and his own favourite literature. He is an authority on seventeenth-century French writers.

Sunday was picnic day, and we cruised the misted waters of Deep Cove Bay to Big and Little Tancook Islands, climbing up and down wharves as he talked familiarly with fishermen and boys cleaning their catch on the boats. Then the ordinary little launch took us to a remote rocky island Eaton had known and loved since childhood. Baskets, blankets, and cushions were unpacked (his farm manager and son were O.C. operations there, as aboard), and a huge standing fire was lighted against a sheer rock wall that isolated our strip of rocky beach.

I tramped the farm with Eaton, who identified every tree and shrub; helped Anne, in her wheelchair, feed the flocks of Canada geese, now year-round residents, that gathered around like farm chickens, taking food from our hands.

Here, indeed, was a rich man — with a wealth of vision, integrity, and spirit, too.

Twenty-Three

The best story? It's the ultimate one always just around the corner or over the bend of the world. Like the answer I've had from so many people in the theatre — Laurence Olivier, Arthur Hill, Maureen Stapleton, Jason Robards. Their finest portrayal? Always the next one. That's what makes an artist or writer — the challenge of excellence yet to be achieved. Certainly it is true in all these cases, as superb performers grow from role to role.

I was talking with Gary Lautens, *The Toronto Star*'s humorist columnist, about why we tackle each new assignment with zeal to do better. "Because," he said quickly, "when you stop getting excited about tomorrow's piece, you're dead." True. The best reporters I've known go as fresh and hard-driving at each new story as though it were their first. What is this crazy fascination — nay, compulsion — about the newspaper business?

I've been in magazine, radio, public relations, and television. None offered the secret satisfaction gained from watching someone on a bus or plane, in a coffee shop or hotel lobby, reading my story, with my by-line, in a big metropolitan daily. Ephemeral? Left on the bench, spread to harbour rubbers in the hallway after rain? Out with the garbage? Ah, but it's also my version in hard print of what happened to people and the world they inhabit during the hours just written off their lives.

You have to be a word person. To me a few words can paint a thousand pictures. Churchill's "blood, sweat and tears"; the Bible's "Jesus wept"; McCrea's "In Flanders fields the poppies blow between the crosses row on row"; "Life, liberty, and the pursuit of happiness"; Roosevelt's "freedom from fear itself" — a handful of words conjuring up whole periods and situations in the history of mankind. Today's colourful jargon can carry a picture-book of messages. "Are you all right?" between lovers, parent and child, friends. "Have a good day." "Take care, eh?" "The Medium Is the Message." Or the distillation into a ten-word critique of an inept performance of a big-name actress, as Dorothy Parker once did in her memorable, "Miss Hepburn ran the gamut of emotion from A to B."

So a good reporter is hung up on words and sweats to make them powerful messengers in a record of the passing scene. Television, by its very nature, must be selective, and thus often exclusive of important implications and parenthetical action away from the camera's eye. (I am speaking now of news and the real world of happenings, not fiction.) Radio, as I learned as an editor in the C.B.C. newsroom, is composed largely of exclamatory headlines followed by briefs. The newspaper, on the other hand, is a great catalogue of human merchandise, with hidden ingredients noted on the packages. It is as uncontrived as is the weird and wonderful everyday passage of events.

I tried to express some of this when my newspaper held a series of sessions for heads of departments. Those in which I was involved were designed to give other branches of the company, the big nine-tenths of operation apart from the newsroom, some insight into our segment. (The newspaper is, to my knowledge, the only mass product of contemporary times built from a reporter's pencil, a photographer's camera, an advertising writer's or artist's concept, through an involved series of operations, including those of the fabulous rolling presses, to home or street delivery in hundreds of thousands every day; and then, destroyed every night, with a whole new enormous output started all over again for the next twenty-four hours.)

In our session, the editor-in-chief, managing editor, associate managing editor, chief editorial writer, and this low person on the totem pole, a reporter, were expositors. After a comprehensive picture of newsroom function by the mandarins, I came on as tail-off — a fitting place, I suggested, since reporters are, indeed, the tail that wags the dog. It's a very long tail, at times, extended to far and unfamiliar places, and nary a news staffer who doesn't feel, on numerous assignments, that it's tied with all the tin cans in every alley.

For despite some team coverage on big news stories, it is basically a lonely one-person business, and you'd better like it that way. Pad, pencil, and typewriter, expense money and a target. And baby, it's cold outside once you leave home office. On out-of-town assignment, nobody's going to hold your hand when quick decisions must be made, with seconds ticking away to an immutable deadline. So you must be able to find that kind of pressure stimulating, and, indeed, the very fuel that fires your energies into high gear and steady mileage. The final night of a big story, when all the copy's in, is one of marked relaxation for ladies and gentlemen of the press, who usually spend it in letting off steam among their own kind.

On one such occasion, in little Prince Edward Island, Ray Timson, now associate managing editor of the *Star,* had headed up a successful and productive *Star* team for a royal tour. We were at leisure until the next afternoon's plane flight, and so photographers, reporters, *et al*, followed Ray to what was then Charlottetown's only late-night club. It was for members only, but Ray always made contacts and led his troops to the rather dingy rooms upstairs.

I happened to be the only female in our group, and somehow we hit on this silly gag of everyone giving me their cash for each new round of drinks. "Give the check to Lotie," they'd say, and the little waitress became more and more upset at the thought that the lady was paying all the shots.

I looked at her innocently. "Don't you do that here in Prince Edward Island? In Toronto, we girls couldn't get men to take us out unless we paid." Her scorn for the males in the party grew with the evening. There was a piano-player who charged ten cents per tune for dancing. We carried on the gag, with me constantly giving her dimes as the men whirled me around.

Next morning, one of our party, en route back from the beer store with a little well-earned libation for our pre-departure sandwich lunch, met the local lady. She was about to pass him with his case of ale when he paused to whisper, "Lotie sent me."

"Well," she said, "you *men* can certainly have Toronto." There's one Islander we saved for the good life in the lovely east, far from the dissolute effeteness of Hogtown.

When you get home from one of the big stories, there may be a smattering of derring-do talk, but most of it is better saved for mother. In the office, it's just another job done. So what did you get out of it? Being part of a real and pulsing world, tuned in on the action, first-hand. You were there, living with a heady, feverish awareness and sensitivity to the basic adventures and misadventures of our time.

Nobody talks much about the digging and the waiting, because it's just part of the story, too. I think of one Democratic convention in Atlantic City, when I was assigned to work under the direction of our *Star* Washington bureau chief, Martin Goodman. Not unexpectedly, foreign staffers drew accommodation far from the crowded convention centre in the city. You have to accept it philosophically. The same thing happens to outlanders when they come to Canada or any other country; home press gets first choice. I remember Dorothy Kilgallen's fury at being billeted at a pokey little hotel in Ottawa away from the main scene.

"This could never happen in the United States," protested the American syndicated gossip columnist.

"Oh yes, Miss Kilgallen," I countered, "it does to *us*."

I didn't offer to share my hotel room with her, as I once did with rival Canadian reporter, Phyllis Griffith, in Trois Rivières, Quebec, at the funeral of Premier Maurice Duplessis. It was a tiny motel room. Phyl's accommodation (for *The Toronto Telegram*) got snafued, and we were friends, although fierce rivals professionally. (She later returned the favour when I was similarly distressed in Montreal.) Without having to discuss it at all, Phyl would go into the tiny bathroom and shut the door tight while I telephoned my story to the *Star*. I followed suit while she telephoned, aware I was much the loser, as she was one of the finest reporters on the continent. As these stories were filed, of frequent necessity in the small hours of the morning, it was much too late for either of us to go outside the single-unit building.

I'd had a frightening lesson in that regard once in Lubec, Maine. Mrs. Lyndon Johnson had come to Campobello with a group of U.S. politicos to meet Mrs. Lester B. Pearson and her party and jointly declare the island an international park. It had been the summer home of the Franklin Roosevelts and scene of the president's crippling illness. Mrs. Johnson's press secretary Liz Carpenter fended me off throughout the ceremonies. But when the American party was set to depart by small boat for the mainland, Mrs. Johnson and her group in one, the U.S. press people in another, I leapt from the wharf into the Johnson craft as it was pulling out. Liz helplessly shook her fist from the other. I nearly didn't make it, but I'd had immersion in the line of duty before.

Anyway, I got back to the little motel, wrote my story in a filmy negligee, then found that the manager had departed and locked the door to the only telephone. *Star* photographer Norm James had long since bedded down in his nearby cabin. However, I had noted a wayside telephone booth along the dirt road at some distance, and so I rushed out, change purse and copy in hand. It wasn't until I was in the middle of dictating my story that I observed a pair of sleazy-looking male characters attracted by the see-through attire of a female at 3.30 a.m. spotlighted in the booth. They were slithering closer. I dropped the phone, screamed, and ran like lightning across a rock and stubble field to Norm's cabin, pounding on the door. Sleepily but uncomplainingly (he'd been partnering reporters around the world for decades), the photographer put on his dressing-gown and escorted me back to the booth.

The prowlers had vanished. I called Toronto again. "We were cut off?" the night editor queried.

"Yup," I said. "Quote: and then Ladybird told me how Lyndon liked to sound out some of his thinking on knotty national and international problems on her, although, of course, she was never the decision maker. . .etc. . .etc. . .etc."

Back to Atlantic City, the Democratic convention, and the little motel. Janice Goodman had come along with her husband, and the only available accommodation for the three of us was a two-bedroom suite with single bathroom. It was a case of me going through their bedroom to the bathroom or vice versa. Naturally, I suggested they take the back bedroom and come through mine.

We had had a very long day and evening, and all our copy was filed. It must have been close to four o'clock when I was awakened by a shaft of light as Janice slipped quietly through my room. I glanced back at the open door and there, with newspapers spread all over the floor, was a kneeling, concentrating bureau chief doing his after-hours homework. Goodman now is editor-in-chief of *The Toronto Star* and still an ace reporter.

Of course, you suffer — particularly when a deskman slashes deathless creations to ribbons; or when a typesetter or telegraph operator or telephone recorder fouls up.

The biggest battles I've seen in the newsrooms of papers I've served have been over use or misuse of stories and pictures, as photographers, critics, reporters, and columnists see it. A hardpressed head writer can alter the import of a story. A changed word can be misleading. Staffers are quick to take umbrage and be vocal about it. I've seen a top critic livid about a changed phrase and columnists resign over a disputed piece. The only time I ever offered my own notice in haste and anger was when some material was added without my knowledge to a story under my name; I felt the added information brought unwarranted and unnecessary disgrace to someone. It was straightened out, and I stayed on. Newspaper people are, as I said, a strange breed. The case involved an old woman who spoke little English and whose name wouldn't be know to a dozen people.

On occasion when a strike involving the editorial department threatens, the Newspaper Guild, our trade union, uses as a weapon against the publisher the right of by-liners to have their names deleted from their output. This can take away from the paper's individuality. I've been among those pressured by the Guild to do this three times, and I've done it twice, but it's a toughie. Not, I think, just because the by-line brings its owner accreditation and identity (as well as responsibility), but because the ties are so close, often, that the effect is almost a personal disorientation as well as a professional blackout.

It's a kind of ''worth'' thing — a regular affirmation that you do exist and somewhere contribute according to your lights. Some of the best reporters I know groan and gnash their teeth over how badly copy is going and what terrible stories they are writing. These tend to be the front-page producers.

Another characteristic of the breed I found, to my amusement, is true of reporters around the world. This was when I was on a press jet in the United States, part of an international group covering Nikita Khrushchev's first visit to America. I edged over to a little klatsch in one corner. There should be valuable pickings here, I thought, for among them were two top men from *The New York Times,* James Reston and Harrison Salisbury, and the leaders of the *Isvestia* and *Pravda* corps, along with some others.

They were deep in heated conversation. The subject? Same as always — what lousy press arrangements! How difficult to get to the people and functions essential to operation, the abomination of pooled coverage, and so on.

It seems to surprise young people who come seeking information about journalism as a possible life work when you talk of speed of output, discipline, stamina, and particularly a compulsive fascination with the news. What did you read in the papers last week or the week before? Did you analyze it to see what it contained and how it was handled? Do you pick up newspapers as soon as you arrive in a new town or city? For here is a reflection of what that place is like, in its gut and bone, as nothing else is. Study the day's editions. What do they play in front-page news? (In Los Angeles, film and television stars, their achievements and problems, are featured as nowhere else; Washington and Ottawa are, of course, highly politically oriented, and so on.)

How does the local paper treat crime? International news (which reveals either world-mindedness or insularity)? Each page, including the advertisements, reflects the immediate concerns and colour of that place. Are there more employment wanted ads than help wanted? What are the city government people arguing about? Strikes? Is social news still considered worthy of purple prosery? How much are eggs and meat and houses and cars and rental apartments? What are people writing about in letters to the editor? — a sensitive community weathervane.

All this is vital, and unless you are vitally interested, go back to the bland, canned product of so much of television, which has so little to say to and about the basic concerns of real people in real places.

The biggest stories are yet to be written, with the greatest need for honest, informed reporting and assessment. There are global problems for which global solutions must be found, if humans are to outlast the century, the growing closeness of a universe of which we are so small and puzzling a part. (Remember Mildred Merryman's lines about the future of the city of Chicago, bursting in importance? "You will still be just a scar, on a little, lonely star.")

There is the new science of prodding the whole inner workings of human beings, to see what we really are, how we can relate to others, and find full expression in ourselves.

There's the mystery of time, the old dimension of which we have learned so little. A philosophical professor said to me: "All the growing research into ageing, genes, effect of environment, are really the first studies of the measurement of time itself. We have shunned that, because death is an ultimate part of time and we are afraid of death."

What answers I have found, in this long and exhilarating life, are dim signposts to more and more questions. And maybe that's what they mean by the old saw, a nose for news. So I hope, too, the next stories I have a crack at are the best ones. Time now to write "30" to this rare indulgence in backtracking.

I can't go along with Will Rogers, who said he'd never met a man he didn't like. But I've rarely met anyone who didn't have a story or an idea that sent me on some fresh trail or led to new comprehension. And that will be my bag, so long as the Dempsey kid keeps running the show.